Elevating Education

A Servant Leadership Approach for Online Educators

Elevating Education: A Servant Leadership Approach for Online Educators

BY

David McNamee

This is a work of creative nonfiction. Some parts have been fictionalized in varying degrees for various purposes.

Copyright © David McNamee, 2025

ISBN: 979-8-9929620-2-4

All rights reserved. No part of this book may be reproduced in any form by any electronic or mechanical means, including information storage and retrieval systems, without permission in writing from the publisher, except by a reviewer who may quote brief passages in a review.

Publisher: Sage Quill Press, LLC

First edition

Disclaimer:

This book is intended for educational and informational purposes only. While it draws on real-world practices and scholarly concepts, certain narratives, examples, and descriptions have been fictionalized or adapted for clarity, emphasis, or illustrative purposes.

The views and interpretations presented are those of the author and do not necessarily reflect those of any institution, organization, or individual mentioned or implied.

This work is not intended to provide legal, medical, or psychological advice. Readers should consult appropriate professionals for advice suited to their specific circumstances.

Names, characters, institutions, and scenarios may be composites or entirely fictitious.

While every precaution has been taken in the preparation of this book, the publisher assumes no responsibility for errors or omissions, or for damages resulting from the use of the information contained herein.

Table of Contents:

Disclaimer: 3

Table of Contents: 4

Introduction 8

    The Evolving Landscape of Higher Education and Leadership Needs 8

    The Leadership Gap in Online Learning Spaces 13

    How Faculty Shape Leadership Mindsets—Even Asynchronously 19

    Purpose and Scope of This Book 23

    How to Use This Book 25

Chapter 1: Foundations of Servant Leadership 29

    Origins of Servant Leadership: Robert Greenleaf's Legacy 29

    Core Characteristics of Servant Leadership 36

    Servant Leadership vs. traditional leadership models. 43

    Why Servant Leadership Is Uniquely Suited to Online Higher Education 51

Contemporary Applications in Virtual Organizations and Education 59

Chapter 2: Servant Leadership in Online Higher Education 68

The Role of Faculty as Servant Leaders in Asynchronous Environments 68

Servant Leadership Through Course Design, LMS Presence, and Communication 76

Humanizing Online Learning: 86

Examples of Servant Leadership Behaviors in Online Classrooms 94

Chapter 3: Modeling Leadership Through Online Course Design and Communication 105

Designing Leadership-Infused Syllabi and LMS Structures 106

Course Announcements as Leadership Moments 114

Board Facilitation Techniques That Build Leadership Values 118

Model Empathy and Active Listening 126

Inclusive, Community-Building Practices in Grading and Feedback 130

Case Examples: Course Announcements and LMS Design Screenshots 133

Chapter 4: Asynchronous Student Leadership Development Activities 141

Structuring Discussion Forums with Rotating Peer Leaders 142

What Are Student-Led Reflection Threads? 146

Leadership Roles in Group Projects 155

Peer Mentoring Programs Within Courses 164

Online leadership reflection journals or blogs. 169

Mock Crisis-Response Simulations 170

Example Activity Templates and Assessment Rubrics..179

Chapter 5: Faculty Self-Assessment and Reflection 184

Why Faculty Self-Awareness Matters in Leadership Modeling 185

Servant Leadership Self-Assessment Tools 192

Reflection prompts for online faculty. 196

Creating a Personal Servant Leadership Development Plan 199

Chapter 6: Resources, Tools, and Templates for Immediate Use 211

    Servant Leadership Reading and Video Resources 212

    Activity and Assignment Instructions 221

    Student Leadership Self-Assessment and Reflection Forms 222

Chapter 7: Voices from the Field: Faculty and Leadership Educator Perspectives 225

    Case Studies 226

    Key Takeaways, Strategies, and Leadership Moments .236

Conclusion 238

Appendix 241

About the Author 250

About Sage Quill Press 250

Also by David McNamee 251

Introduction

As higher education rapidly shifts toward digital platforms, the need for effective leadership has become more critical than ever. Online learning environments require more than subject expertise—they demand strong relational and adaptive leadership that can support diverse, remote learners. Faculty members, often the primary point of contact in virtual classrooms, play a vital leadership role in shaping student engagement, motivation, and success.

Traditional top-down leadership models are proving insufficient in this evolving context. Instead, models like servant leadership—which emphasize empathy, student-centeredness, and personal development—offer a more relevant and impactful approach. Developing leadership skills in educators is no longer optional; it is essential for fostering inclusive, responsive, and meaningful learning experiences in the digital age.

The Evolving Landscape of Higher Education and Leadership Needs

Higher education is undergoing one of the most profound transformations in its history. Over the past few decades, technological innovation, shifting student demographics, and the globalization of education have radically reshaped how, when, and where learning takes place. Among the most significant changes is the meteoric rise of online education, which has transcended geographical boundaries and created new avenues for access, inclusion, and innovation in teaching and learning.

This digital revolution has not merely altered the mode of delivery; it has fundamentally disrupted the traditional assumptions about what leadership looks like in academic institutions. Where leadership was once associated primarily with formal administrative roles and hierarchical decision-making structures, today's educational environment calls for more distributed, relational, and responsive forms of leadership. The need for a paradigm shift is particularly urgent in online education, where the dynamics of engagement, communication, and influence operate very differently than in face-to-face settings.

In conventional campus-based models, leadership was often exercised in person, through meetings, speeches, and visible day-to-day presence. In contrast, the virtual campus demands leadership that is less about physical visibility and more about relational presence, clarity of communication, cultural responsiveness, and emotional intelligence. Faculty, once viewed mainly as conveyors of content, now play a far more expansive role. In the absence of physical proximity, they become the primary human connection for students navigating an otherwise digital and potentially isolating academic journey.

This shift has placed new expectations on faculty members—not only to be content experts and skilled educators but also to embody leadership in ways that resonate with the challenges and opportunities of online learning. They are called upon to foster trust, promote engagement, support student well-being, and create inclusive virtual learning environments where all students can thrive. This emerging reality has elevated the importance of a leadership model that prioritizes human connection, empathy, adaptability, and service.

The Rise of Servant Leadership in Online Education

Enter servant leadership—a philosophy and practice of leadership that flips traditional power dynamics on their head. Coined by Robert K. Greenleaf in the 1970s, servant leadership centers on the idea that the primary role of a leader is to serve others, nurturing their growth, potential, and autonomy. In the context of online higher education, this model is especially relevant. It aligns with the need for student-centered teaching approaches and highlights the importance of listening, empathy, healing, stewardship, and community-building—qualities that directly contribute to meaningful online learning experiences.

Unlike directive or authoritarian styles that may work in rigid institutional hierarchies, servant leadership fosters collaboration, mutual respect, and empowerment. It sees leadership not as a status to be wielded but as a relationship to be nurtured. For faculty leading online courses, this model offers a powerful lens through which to reimagine their role—not just as knowledge transmitters, but as transformational figures in students' academic and personal development.

Servant leadership also provides a framework for institutions to rethink how they support their educators. As online programs expand, there is a growing need for faculty development initiatives that go beyond technical training and delve into the interpersonal, emotional, and ethical dimensions of leadership. By cultivating servant leadership qualities, institutions can better prepare faculty to lead in ways that are authentic, inclusive, and effective across diverse learning environments.

Redefining Leadership Beyond Administration

One of the most crucial implications of this new leadership paradigm is that leadership in higher education is no longer the sole domain of those in official administrative roles. In today's interconnected academic ecosystem, leadership is a shared responsibility. Faculty, instructional designers, support staff, and even students themselves are all potential leaders who contribute to the educational experience and institutional culture.

This democratization of leadership is particularly evident in online learning, where traditional barriers of rank and role are often less visible. Faculty who embrace a servant leadership mindset are better positioned to build trust, foster resilience, and create a sense of belonging among their students—many of whom may be juggling complex lives, careers, and responsibilities outside of school. They become mentors, role models, and co-learners, modeling the very values—such as empathy, integrity, and perseverance—that they aim to instill.

In this redefined landscape, leadership is not an external mantle but an internal orientation. It is about showing up with intentionality, modeling ethical behavior, and nurturing the potential in others. It's about guiding students not just to academic success, but to personal growth and civic responsibility.

As the higher education sector continues to evolve in response to digital disruption and global complexity, the call for thoughtful, values-driven leadership has never been more urgent. Online education, with its unique challenges and possibilities, provides a powerful context in which to cultivate and practice servant leadership. Institutions that recognize and invest in the leadership development of their faculty will not only enhance the quality of their online programs but also foster a more compassionate, adaptive, and effective academic culture.

The Leadership Gap in Online Learning Spaces

Despite the growing recognition of the critical role leadership plays in online education, a significant and often overlooked gap persists. This leadership gap is not about the absence of formal authority or institutional structure. Rather, it lies in the lack of preparation, support, and intentional development of the relational and adaptive leadership capacities required for success in virtual learning environments.

As online education continues to grow in scope, scale, and significance, the limitations of traditional faculty training models become increasingly apparent. Most online instructors enter their roles well-versed in subject matter expertise and, at best, equipped with basic training on using learning management systems (LMS), grading tools, and digital content delivery. However, the more nuanced and vital aspects of leadership—such as fostering engagement, building community, supporting student well-being, and cultivating trust—are often treated as peripheral, if addressed at all.

This gap has tangible consequences. The absence of strong relational leadership in online classrooms contributes directly to student disengagement, low retention rates, and poor academic outcomes. Unlike traditional face-to-face settings, where nonverbal cues, spontaneous conversations, and physical presence can foster a sense of connection, online students frequently report feelings of isolation, detachment, and anonymity. Many students never interact with faculty in real-time, and asynchronous communication can feel impersonal without deliberate relational efforts. When instructors lack the leadership training to humanize these digital interactions, students can become disengaged, discouraged, or disoriented—especially those from underrepresented or non-traditional backgrounds.

The leadership gap is also evident in the way institutions structure their support for online faculty. In many cases, instructors operate in siloed environments, disconnected from broader institutional goals or peer networks. This decentralization can be especially pronounced for adjunct or part-time faculty, who often teach multiple courses across institutions and have little access to mentoring or community-building opportunities. Without mechanisms for peer collaboration, shared reflection, or leadership coaching, faculty may find it difficult to develop a cohesive vision for their teaching or to align with the institution's mission in meaningful ways.

Furthermore, this lack of leadership support and recognition is compounded by systemic issues in the way higher education evaluates faculty performance. Traditional metrics—such as publication records, student satisfaction scores, or course completion rates—tend to privilege research output and surface-level indicators of teaching effectiveness. Rarely do these measures capture the intangible but essential leadership behaviors that contribute to student success in online spaces: empathy, adaptability, relational attentiveness, and the ability to foster inclusive learning communities.

The misalignment between institutional evaluation systems and the realities of online teaching creates a discouraging paradox. Faculty are expected to perform increasingly complex roles in digital classrooms—facilitating learning, supporting diverse student needs, managing technology, and embodying institutional values—yet they are rarely given the training, time, or incentives to develop the leadership capacities necessary to do so effectively. As a result, even well-intentioned educators can find themselves unprepared for the interpersonal and emotional demands of online teaching.

This leadership gap is not simply a faculty-level issue—it reflects deeper cultural and structural challenges within higher education. For decades, the dominant narrative has equated leadership with authority, administration, or managerial control. Faculty, particularly those in non-tenure-track or online positions, have often been viewed as content deliverers rather than as transformative leaders. Reimagining this narrative is essential if we are to close the leadership gap in online education.

The rise of servant leadership offers a compelling alternative framework. In contrast to traditional top-down models, servant leadership emphasizes collaboration, humility, and a commitment to the growth and well-being of others. This model is especially well-suited to online learning environments, where leadership must be relational rather than positional, and where influence is exercised not through formal titles, but through presence, responsiveness, and intentional care.

Servant leadership encourages faculty to see themselves as stewards of students' holistic development—not just intellectual achievement, but also personal growth, confidence, and resilience. This approach demands a shift in mindset: from instructor to guide, from authority figure to mentor, from content expert to co-learner. It also requires concrete skills: active listening, empathetic communication, cultural responsiveness, and a capacity to build community across digital platforms.

Bridging the leadership gap, therefore, begins with a fundamental rethinking of faculty development. Institutions must move beyond basic LMS training and invest in comprehensive leadership education that equips instructors to navigate the relational and emotional dimensions of online teaching. Workshops, certificate programs, coaching, and peer learning communities can all play a role in cultivating the servant leadership mindset. Moreover, these initiatives should not be optional or isolated—they must be embedded into the broader institutional culture and reinforced through recognition, rewards, and accountability structures.

Professional development programs must also be tailored to the realities of online faculty work. This includes addressing the challenges of asynchronous communication, fostering student motivation in self-paced environments, managing digital fatigue, and leveraging technology to build authentic human connections. Leadership development must not only offer theory but also practical strategies, examples, and tools that educators can implement immediately in their classrooms.

Equally important is the creation of structures that support ongoing reflection and growth. Leadership is not a one-time skill to be acquired but a continuous practice to be nurtured. Institutions should foster cultures of shared leadership, where faculty have opportunities to collaborate, share insights, and collectively shape the educational experience. Mentorship programs, teaching fellowships, and online faculty learning circles can all contribute to a more connected and empowered academic workforce.

Additionally, evaluation systems must evolve to recognize and reward leadership behaviors. Institutions should develop new metrics that value relational teaching, community building, and student support—especially in the online context. Student feedback tools can be redesigned to capture the impact of faculty leadership on engagement and belonging, not just content delivery or grading turnaround. Promotion and tenure criteria should reflect the multifaceted nature of teaching excellence, including leadership in virtual learning spaces.

Finally, closing the leadership gap is not just about faculty; it's about vision. Senior administrators and academic leaders must model the servant leadership principles they seek to instill. Institutional change requires alignment at all levels—policies, practices, culture, and mindset. Leaders who prioritize people over processes, who listen before they command, and who lead by serving can set the tone for a more human-centered, values-driven approach to online education.

How Faculty Shape Leadership Mindsets— Even Asynchronously

One of the most powerful yet often underestimated aspects of online education is the potential for faculty to shape and nurture leadership mindsets in students—even in asynchronous learning environments. While the absence of real-time interaction is sometimes perceived as a limitation, it can actually create space for deeper engagement, intentional design, and reflective learning. When approached thoughtfully, asynchronous teaching becomes a powerful medium for modeling and fostering the principles of leadership, especially servant leadership.

In traditional classroom settings, leadership development often emerges through direct mentorship, classroom discussions, and spontaneous interactions. However, in asynchronous environments, the influence of faculty is more subtle—but no less profound. Every aspect of a course's design and delivery becomes a touchpoint through which leadership values can be communicated and reinforced. The tone of announcements, the nature of assignments, the structure of discussions, and the clarity of expectations all serve as indirect yet potent messages about what kind of leadership is encouraged and modeled.

Faculty who approach their teaching with a servant leadership mindset—prioritizing empathy, inclusion, growth, and service—can effectively embed these values into the online learning experience. This begins with course design. A course built around collaboration rather than competition, with clear instructions, accessible resources, and opportunities for student voice, inherently communicates that the instructor values equity and shared responsibility. These are foundational aspects of servant leadership.

For instance, when a faculty member provides timely, thoughtful, and personalized feedback on assignments, it signals respect for the student's effort and a commitment to their individual growth. This seemingly routine task becomes an act of leadership modeling. It teaches students that leadership involves attentiveness, encouragement, and a belief in the potential of others.

Similarly, asynchronous discussion forums—when carefully curated—can become vibrant spaces for intellectual leadership and peer learning. When faculty set expectations that encourage inclusive dialogue, respectful disagreement, and thoughtful inquiry, they create a space where leadership skills such as active listening, empathy, and ethical reasoning can flourish. By participating meaningfully in these forums, faculty demonstrate how to elevate the conversation, recognize diverse perspectives, and engage with ideas respectfully. These practices, when repeated and reinforced, shape the student's understanding of what good leadership looks and feels like.

Responding to student challenges with compassion and flexibility is another critical aspect. Online learners often juggle multiple responsibilities, such as work, family, and education. When faculty accommodate legitimate needs, offer words of encouragement, or simply acknowledge a student's struggle, they reinforce the idea that leadership is not about rigid control, but about supporting and empowering others. These small moments create a ripple effect—students not only feel seen and supported but are also more likely to mirror those leadership traits in their own interactions.

Asynchronous learning also presents unique opportunities for students to step into leadership roles themselves. Peer-led discussion threads, group projects, and collaborative assignments provide platforms for students to exercise initiative, communicate effectively, and practice team-based leadership. Faculty play a vital role in scaffolding these opportunities—setting clear goals, establishing guidelines for respectful collaboration, and encouraging reflection on group dynamics.

One particularly valuable but often underused tool in asynchronous environments is reflective journaling. Unlike the fast-paced exchanges of real-time discussion, journaling invites introspection. Students are encouraged to think critically about their learning experiences, personal values, ethical dilemmas, and evolving beliefs. When these reflections are guided by prompts related to leadership, identity, and service, they become catalysts for self-awareness and growth.

Faculty can further enhance this process by offering meaningful feedback on reflective submissions—not in the form of judgment or evaluation, but as mentorship. Asking thoughtful questions, suggesting further avenues for inquiry, or connecting reflections to course themes can deepen the student's engagement and reinforce the practice of reflection as a leadership discipline.

Importantly, asynchronous settings also help democratize participation. In traditional classrooms, a few confident voices often dominate discussions. But in online forums and written assignments, students have time to think, revise, and express themselves more fully. This format gives introverted or reflective learners a stronger voice, helping them build confidence in their ideas and find their own leadership style.

Finally, it is worth emphasizing that shaping leadership mindsets in an asynchronous context requires consistency. Students pay attention to how faculty show up—whether they follow through on promises, whether their grading is fair and timely, whether they respond respectfully, and whether they embody the same values they expect from students. These small, daily acts of integrity and professionalism create a learning culture that speaks volumes.

Purpose and Scope of This Book

This book was born out of a fundamental recognition: leadership development is not an optional or peripheral goal of higher education—it is central to its mission. In a world defined by rapid change, complexity, and global interdependence, our society urgently needs leaders who are not only knowledgeable but also empathetic, ethical, and committed to the well-being of others. Nowhere is this more relevant—and more overlooked—than in the context of online higher education.

As educators, we often focus on delivering content, managing assessment, and maintaining academic standards. Yet at the heart of our work lies a deeper responsibility: to cultivate human potential. This book contends that every online instructor, regardless of discipline or course level, has the opportunity—and indeed the imperative—to shape the next generation of leaders through intentional teaching practices grounded in servant leadership.

What This Book Aims to Do

The primary purpose of this book is to provide a practical, research-informed framework for integrating servant leadership principles into the design and facilitation of online courses. It is a guide for educators who wish to lead with empathy, foster inclusive communities, and inspire meaningful student growth—even in the absence of face-to-face contact.

This book bridges the gap between theory and practice, offering concrete strategies, actionable tools, and real-world examples to help educators translate abstract leadership values into everyday teaching behaviors. It does not assume a background in leadership studies. Rather, it invites faculty to explore leadership from within their own context—as mentors, guides, and facilitators of learning in virtual environments.

While the core focus is on fully online higher education, the principles explored here are highly adaptable. Educators working in hybrid, blended, or low-residency programs will also find relevant insights. Whether you're teaching undergraduates in general education courses or guiding doctoral candidates in advanced research, the practices presented can enhance your capacity to connect, inspire, and lead.

This book also seeks to elevate the leadership contributions of online faculty, whose influence is often invisible in traditional academic metrics. Too often, leadership in higher education is associated solely with administrative roles or research excellence. This book challenges that narrative by centering the voices and experiences of educators working in virtual spaces. It affirms that faculty leadership is relational, pedagogical, and deeply impactful, especially when enacted with intentionality and care.

How to Use This Book

This book has been designed to be flexible, accessible, and immediately applicable. It can support a variety of professional development goals depending on your role, experience level, and institutional context:

1. Faculty Development Tool

Institutions can use this book as part of structured professional learning for online instructors. Each chapter includes:

- Reflective prompts for self-assessment and group dialogue
- Case studies drawn from real online teaching experiences
- Activity templates that can be used in workshops, faculty retreats, or peer mentoring programs

2. Course Design Aid

For faculty and instructional designers, this book offers **guiding principles for course development and redesign.** Whether you're building a new course from scratch or refining an existing syllabus, the book provides:

- A student-centered framework aligned with servant leadership
- Strategies for fostering engagement, equity, and motivation
- Tips for using learning technologies in values-based ways

3. Mentoring and Peer Support Resource

Experienced educators can use this book as a **mentoring tool** for new or adjunct instructors. The language is accessible, the examples are relatable, and the practices are scalable—making it ideal for supporting meaningful, peer-led conversations about leadership, pedagogy, and professional identity.

Each chapter builds intentionally on the one before it, beginning with foundational definitions of leadership and servant leadership, and moving toward practical, classroom-level implementation. The structure of the book allows for **multiple points of entry:**

- You may choose to read from beginning to end for a comprehensive understanding.
- You may dip into specific chapters to address a particular challenge or question.
- You may return to certain sections over time as your teaching practice evolves.

In addition to core content, the book provides:

- Downloadable tools and templates (e.g., course reflection rubrics, student leadership activity ideas)
- Adaptable leadership development activities suitable for different class sizes and formats

- Curated reading lists, videos, and multimedia resources for deeper exploration

These resources are designed to support ongoing professional growth, whether you are working individually, within a team, or across departments.

Ultimately, this book offers a simple but powerful invitation: To see yourself not just as a content expert, but as a leader. A leader who shapes not only what students know, but how they think, relate, and act in the world.

Whether you are a seasoned online educator or stepping into the virtual classroom for the first time, you have the ability to make a lasting difference. By adopting a servant leadership approach, you can create learning environments that inspire transformation—not just academically, but personally and ethically.

This is not just about better teaching. It's about building a better future—one student, one course, one act of leadership at a time.

Chapter 1: Foundations of Servant Leadership

What does it mean to lead by serving, especially in a world that often equates leadership with authority, control, and visibility? In online higher education, where much of the faculty-student relationship is mediated by technology and distance, this question becomes even more critical. This chapter introduces the foundational philosophy of servant leadership, tracing its origins and key principles, and exploring how it offers a powerful lens for educators navigating the digital classroom.

Origins of Servant Leadership: Robert Greenleaf's Legacy

The concept of *servant leadership* was introduced by Robert K. Greenleaf in his groundbreaking 1970 essay, *The Servant as Leader*.

In a time when traditional leadership models were largely hierarchical—driven by authority, control, and command—Greenleaf offered a radical alternative.

He proposed that the most effective leaders are, first and foremost, **servants**. This was not merely a semantic shift; it was a profound reimagining of leadership as rooted in humility, empathy, and the desire to uplift others.

Greenleaf wrote, *"The servant-leader is servant first... It begins with the natural feeling that one wants to serve, to serve first. Then conscious choice brings one to aspire to lead."*

This idea reversed the conventional order of leadership. Instead of beginning with a quest for power or position, servant leadership begins with **a commitment to others**—to their growth, their well-being, and their autonomy.

A Story That Sparked a Movement

Greenleaf's vision was partially inspired by Herman Hesse's 1932 novella, *Journey to the East*. In the story, a spiritual group sets out on a pilgrimage guided by a humble servant named Leo. Though Leo performs only menial tasks, his quiet wisdom and inner stability hold the group together. When Leo disappears, the expedition disintegrates into chaos. Only later does the narrator realize that Leo was the true leader all along—not through dominance, but through service, presence, and moral integrity.

For Greenleaf, Leo represented a timeless truth: **leadership is not about titles, but about influence born from service.** This metaphor resonated deeply and laid the foundation for what would become a global leadership philosophy.

Principles of Servant Leadership

Over the years, scholars and practitioners have distilled Greenleaf's philosophy into a number of key principles that define the servant leader's mindset and behavior. Among the most widely recognized are:

- **Empathy** – Truly understanding and valuing others' experiences and perspectives
- **Listening** – Giving full attention to others, seeking to understand before being understood
- **Healing** – Recognizing and responding to personal or institutional wounds
- **Awareness** – Being attuned to oneself and the needs of others
- **Persuasion** – Influencing through reason and relationship rather than authority
- **Conceptualization** – Seeing beyond day-to-day realities to envision a better future
- **Foresight** – Anticipating consequences and learning from the past

- **Stewardship** – Holding institutions and resources in trust for the greater good

- **Commitment to the growth of people** – Investing in the personal, professional, and spiritual development of others

- **Building community** – Fostering connection, belonging, and mutual responsibility

These principles are not merely aspirational. They have practical implications for how leaders—especially educators—communicate, make decisions, manage conflict, and structure learning environments.

Relevance to Online Higher Education

While Greenleaf's ideas were conceived in a pre-digital world, their relevance has only grown in today's online educational landscape. Virtual classrooms, asynchronous communication, and distributed learning environments pose unique challenges to traditional leadership. Faculty cannot rely on physical presence, authority by proximity, or real-time charisma. Instead, their influence must come through authenticity, consistency, and care—qualities deeply aligned with servant leadership.

In many ways, online instructors are uniquely positioned to model servant leadership. They are the direct connection between students and the institution, and they often have more flexibility to design learning experiences that reflect inclusive, student-centered values. By adopting a servant-leader mindset, online faculty can transform routine interactions into opportunities for mentorship, empowerment, and ethical modeling.

For example:

- A **thoughtful announcement** can set the tone for a week's worth of learning, signaling that the instructor sees and values students as whole people.

- A **discussion forum prompt** that encourages diverse perspectives or ethical reflection can help students see themselves as emerging leaders.

- **Feedback on assignments**, when delivered with care and encouragement, can communicate belief in a student's potential—often at a moment when it is most needed.

These moments, while small in isolation, accumulate over time to form a leadership presence that is felt even without synchronous interaction.

Servant Leadership as a Way of Being

Perhaps the most transformative insight Greenleaf offered is that servant leadership is not a technique or a management style—it is a way of being. It starts with who we are and how we see the people around us. For educators, this means seeing students not as passive recipients of knowledge, but as full human beings with untapped potential, diverse backgrounds, and unique leadership capacities of their own.

This approach demands intentional self-reflection. Faculty must ask:

- Am I listening deeply to my students?
- Do my course policies and communication reflect care and fairness?
- Am I creating space for student voice and leadership?
- How do I model the values I want students to embody?

These questions help shift the focus from performance to presence, from control to co-creation. And in doing so, they align education with its highest purpose: the development of character, community, and capacity for contribution.

Servant Leadership and Institutional Culture

Greenleaf's work was not limited to individual behavior; he envisioned servant leadership as a principle for institutional transformation. He believed that organizations—including universities—should be designed to serve their people. Leaders at every level, from department chairs to instructional designers to faculty, have a role in shaping systems that reflect justice, empowerment, and compassion.

For online educators, this means advocating not only within the virtual classroom but also within institutional structures:

- Pushing for accessible course design and universal design for learning (UDL)
- Participating in professional development around equity and inclusion
- Supporting policies that value student mental health, flexibility, and holistic success
- Mentoring new instructors with a spirit of generosity and shared growth

Such acts are not always recognized or rewarded in traditional academic metrics, but they are central to building a more humane and effective educational system.

In an era marked by uncertainty, inequity, and digital disruption, servant leadership offers a model that is both timeless and urgently relevant. It speaks to the heart of what education is about: human connection, growth, and transformation.

As faculty members—especially in online settings—we have the opportunity to be servant leaders every day. Through our teaching, our communication, and our presence, we can model a leadership style that is grounded not in control but in compassion; not in hierarchy but in humility.

But it all begins here, with a shift in mindset: from *"What can I teach?"* to *"Whom can I serve?"*

Core Characteristics of Servant Leadership

Greenleaf identified several key characteristics that define servant leaders. These traits are not rigid rules but guiding principles that shape a leader's behavior, mindset, and relationships. In the context of online higher education, these characteristics can be thoughtfully integrated into course design, communication strategies, and pedagogical approaches.

Listening

Listening is the foundation of servant leadership. It involves more than just hearing words; it requires deep, empathetic attention to the needs, concerns, and perspectives of others. For faculty in online environments, listening takes on new forms—through student discussion posts, reflective journals, emails, and feedback forms.

A servant leader listens without judgment, creating space for students to express themselves and feel heard. This can be achieved through active engagement in online forums, thoughtful responses to student inquiries, and openness to feedback. By modeling attentive listening, faculty encourage students to do the same, fostering a culture of mutual respect and understanding.

Empathy

Empathy goes beyond understanding another's situation; it involves sharing in their feelings and experiences. In an online classroom, where nonverbal cues are often absent, faculty must be especially intentional about expressing empathy.

This can involve acknowledging the challenges students face, offering flexibility during difficult times, and personalizing interactions. Empathy builds trust and connection, which are critical for student engagement and success. When students feel that their instructor genuinely cares about their well-being, they are more likely to participate actively and persist through challenges.

Healing

Servant leaders recognize the potential for personal and collective healing in the educational process. Healing involves addressing emotional wounds, fostering resilience, and creating environments where individuals can recover and grow.

In online education, faculty may encounter students dealing with stress, trauma, or self-doubt. By offering supportive feedback, maintaining a nonjudgmental tone, and encouraging self-compassion, instructors can contribute to students' emotional well-being. Faculty can also engage in their own healing by reflecting on their teaching practices, embracing vulnerability, and seeking growth after setbacks.

Awareness

Awareness is the ability to see oneself and others with clarity. It involves understanding personal biases, emotions, and behaviors, as well as being attuned to the dynamics of the learning environment.

Online faculty must cultivate both self-awareness and situational awareness. This includes being mindful of how their words and actions are perceived in digital spaces, recognizing the diversity of student experiences, and adjusting their approach based on context. Awareness also involves staying informed about current events, institutional policies, and issues that affect students' lives.

By modeling awareness, faculty can help students develop their own critical consciousness and ethical sensibilities. This, in turn, fosters a learning community grounded in reflection, respect, and social responsibility.

Persuasion

Unlike coercive forms of authority, servant leadership relies on persuasion to build consensus and inspire action. Persuasion involves articulating a compelling vision, engaging in dialogue, and encouraging voluntary commitment.

In the classroom, faculty can use persuasion to motivate students, promote collaboration, and guide decision-making. This might include presenting multiple perspectives on an issue, encouraging civil discourse, and inviting students to co-create aspects of the course.

By prioritizing persuasion over compliance, faculty empower students to think critically and act autonomously. This not only enhances learning outcomes but also prepares students for ethical leadership in their own spheres of influence.

Conceptualization

Conceptualization is the ability to think beyond day-to-day realities and envision broader possibilities. It involves strategic thinking, imagination, and the capacity to balance short-term needs with long-term goals.

Faculty who embrace conceptualization consider how their courses contribute to students' overall development and societal impact. They design learning experiences that integrate academic content with real-world relevance, ethical considerations, and leadership development.

Conceptual thinking also supports innovation in course design and pedagogy. By imagining new ways to engage students, address challenges, and build community, faculty can transform online education into a dynamic and meaningful journey.

Foresight

Foresight is closely related to conceptualization but focuses specifically on anticipating future outcomes based on past experiences and present realities. It involves strategic judgment, risk assessment, and long-term planning.

In an online course, foresight enables faculty to anticipate student needs, identify potential obstacles, and design proactive solutions. For example, an instructor might provide clear guidelines and FAQs to preempt confusion, or build in check-in points to monitor student progress.

Foresight also supports the cultivation of resilience and adaptability. By modeling thoughtful decision-making and preparing students for future challenges, faculty contribute to their leadership readiness and personal growth.

Stewardship

Stewardship involves taking responsibility for the well-being of the organization and those within it. It reflects a commitment to serving the greater good, using resources wisely, and upholding ethical standards.

Online faculty act as stewards of their courses, their students' learning journeys, and the broader educational mission. This includes maintaining academic integrity, promoting inclusive practices, and advocating for equitable access to education.

Stewardship also extends to self-care and professional development. Faculty must manage their time and energy responsibly, seek opportunities for growth, and contribute to a culture of excellence and collaboration.

Commitment to the Growth of Others

At the heart of servant leadership is a deep commitment to the personal, academic, and professional growth of others.

This goes beyond delivering content to fostering students' holistic development.

Faculty demonstrate this commitment by providing constructive feedback, mentoring students, and creating opportunities for leadership and self-discovery. They recognize and nurture each student's potential, offering encouragement and guidance along the way.

This commitment also involves challenging students to stretch their thinking, reflect on their values, and pursue meaningful goals. When faculty invest in their students' growth, they help cultivate the next generation of ethical, compassionate, and effective leaders.

Building Community

Servant leaders are community builders. They create environments where individuals feel connected, valued, and supported. In online education, where physical distance can lead to feelings of isolation, building community is especially important.

Faculty can foster community through intentional course design, inclusive communication, and collaborative learning activities. Techniques such as introductory videos, peer discussions, and group projects help establish a sense of belonging and shared purpose.

Community building also involves cultivating a classroom culture rooted in respect, openness, and mutual support. When students feel part of a learning community, they are more likely to engage fully, support one another, and achieve their goals.

The foundations of servant leadership provide a powerful framework for educators seeking to lead with integrity, compassion, and purpose in online higher education.

By embracing the principles articulated by Robert Greenleaf and applying them in thoughtful, context-specific ways, faculty can transform their virtual classrooms into spaces of growth, connection, and transformation. In doing so, they not only enrich their students' learning experiences but also contribute to a more humane and equitable educational landscape.

Servant Leadership vs. traditional leadership models.

Understanding the distinctions between servant leadership and traditional leadership models is essential for educators seeking to reshape the dynamics of teaching and learning— especially in online environments where leadership must be intentional, relational, and values-driven. These two paradigms are not simply different management styles; they reflect fundamentally different beliefs about power, purpose, and human development.

Traditional Leadership:

Traditional leadership models have long dominated corporate, governmental, and educational institutions. Rooted in industrial-era management theories such as Taylorism and Scientific Management, these models emphasize efficiency, control, and hierarchy. Leadership is often conceived as a top-down process, where authority flows from the top of the organizational pyramid to the bottom. Leaders are positioned as commanders—those who set the direction, make decisions, and ensure compliance among subordinates.

In these models, success is typically measured by quantifiable outcomes: increased productivity, higher profitability, faster turnaround times, or elevated academic performance metrics such as test scores, graduation rates, and institutional rankings. The individual's role—whether employee, student, or subordinate—is often defined in terms of how well they contribute to the organization's predefined goals.

This framework tends to prioritize:

- Compliance over creativity
- Stability over adaptability

- Uniformity over individualization
- Authority over empathy

In practice, traditional leadership can result in rigid structures that stifle innovation and suppress voice. It may discourage risk-taking, hinder collaboration, and foster environments where fear of failure outweighs the pursuit of learning or growth. While such models may function effectively in systems that require strict coordination—such as military organizations or certain manufacturing sectors—they are less aligned with the complex, human-centered nature of education.

Servant Leadership: A Human-Centered Alternative

Servant leadership offers a compelling counterpoint. First articulated by Robert Greenleaf in the 1970s, this model places service to others at the core of leadership. Instead of asking, *"How can others help me achieve my goals?"*, the servant leader asks, *"How can I help others reach their fullest potential?"* Leadership, in this view, is not about commanding or managing others, but about enabling and empowering them.

The servant leader leads not from above, but from among and beside. Their focus is not on accumulating power but on distributing it in ways that build capacity and foster autonomy.

Influence arises not from position or authority, but from credibility, trustworthiness, and relational depth.

Key Contrasts Between Traditional and Servant Leadership

Element	Traditional Leadership	Servant Leadership
Power Source	Hierarchical position	Moral authority and service
Primary Goal	Organizational success	Individual and collective growth
View of People	Resources to manage	People to nurture and empower
Decision-Making	Top-down, directive	Participatory, consensus-driven
Communication Style	Instructional, one-way	Dialogic, reflective, inclusive
Motivation	Compliance and efficiency	Commitment, purpose, and care

| Ethical Stance | May be neutral or utilitarian | Explicitly moral and value-driven |

These distinctions are not merely theoretical—they play out in everyday interactions and decisions.

Consider how a traditional leader might respond to a student who fails to meet a deadline, likely by enforcement of policy or penalty. A servant leader, by contrast, would begin with inquiry and compassion: *"What's going on in your life right now, and how can I support you?"*

This doesn't mean lowering standards or avoiding accountability. Servant leadership still values excellence and expects responsibility. However, it seeks to achieve those outcomes through care, trust, and mutual respect, rather than fear or obligation.

The Moral and Ethical Foundation of Servant Leadership

One of the most powerful distinctions between traditional and servant leadership is ethical orientation. Traditional models often adopt a value-neutral or utilitarian stance: whatever achieves the goal most efficiently is justified. In contrast, servant leadership is rooted in ethical intentionality. It upholds justice, dignity, transparency, and stewardship as non-negotiable components of leadership.

Greenleaf emphasized that the central question of servant leadership is this:

"Do those served grow as persons? Do they, while being served, become healthier, wiser, freer, more autonomous, more likely themselves to become servants?"

This criterion elevates the purpose of leadership from transactional to transformational. It is not enough to produce outcomes; the process by which outcomes are achieved must also cultivate human flourishing. In educational contexts, this ethical grounding has profound implications. It suggests that how we teach—how we lead our classrooms—matters just as much as what we teach.

Reframing Faculty and Student Roles

In traditional academic models, faculty are often positioned as experts and authorities whose primary responsibility is to transmit knowledge. Students are passive recipients, expected to absorb, reproduce, and conform. This arrangement mirrors traditional leadership dynamics: the leader holds the knowledge and power, while the follower complies.

Servant leadership invites a different paradigm. Here, faculty are seen as facilitators of growth, and students as active participants with unique experiences, perspectives, and potential. The classroom becomes a relational space, not a transactional one. Learning is not simply about information delivery, but about transformation—intellectual, emotional, and ethical.

In this framework:

- Feedback becomes dialogue, not judgment.

- Assessments are opportunities for reflection, not just evaluation.

- Policies are designed with compassion and equity, not control and uniformity.

- Authority is used not to dominate, but to elevate.

Such a model is especially powerful in online environments, where the absence of physical proximity requires greater intentionality in communication, community-building, and trust. Servant leadership can humanize digital education by foregrounding presence, empathy, and responsiveness.

A Shift in Metrics and Measures

The contrast between servant and traditional leadership also calls into question how we measure success. Traditional models often focus on metrics: grades, completion rates, standardized test scores, or institutional rankings. While these data points have value, they offer an incomplete picture of what meaningful learning and development entail.

Servant leadership encourages broader, deeper metrics of success:

- Student engagement and agency
- Moral development and ethical reasoning
- Sense of belonging and psychological safety
- Capacity for collaboration, empathy, and critical thinking

These outcomes are harder to quantify, but they are no less vital. In fact, they are essential to the kind of leadership our world increasingly needs—especially in an age marked by complexity, interdependence, and moral uncertainty.

The decision to embrace servant leadership in education is not a matter of style or preference—it is a philosophical commitment. It requires us to critically examine our assumptions about power, purpose, and people. It invites us to ask not only *what kind of educators we want to be,* but *what kind of human beings we want to become*—and what kind of world we want to help build.

Why Servant Leadership Is Uniquely Suited to Online Higher Education

In recent years, online higher education has transformed from a niche offering into a mainstream modality, serving millions of students worldwide. While its flexibility and accessibility offer significant benefits, the online learning environment also presents unique challenges that can hinder student engagement, persistence, and academic success. Servant leadership, with its deep focus on empathy, empowerment, and relationship-building, offers a powerful and timely response to these challenges.

More than a leadership theory, servant leadership is a philosophy of practice—a way of being that centers the needs of others and aims to foster their growth and development. In online education, where distance, autonomy, and technological mediation can complicate the relational dynamics of teaching and learning, this philosophy is not only applicable—it is essential.

1. Addressing the Relational Gap in Online Learning

One of the most frequently cited challenges of online education is the absence of physical presence. In traditional classrooms, instructors and students share a physical space that enables spontaneous interactions, nonverbal communication, and a general sense of community. These subtle yet powerful cues—eye contact, body language, shared laughter, or even the passing of a handout—create relational bonds and reinforce a shared learning experience.

In contrast, the online classroom, particularly in asynchronous formats, often lacks these immediacies. Students may feel disconnected, invisible, or like passive observers rather than engaged participants. This detachment can negatively impact motivation, mental health, and academic performance.

Servant leadership addresses this relational gap through its core commitment to empathy, listening, and authentic connection. Faculty who adopt this model in the online space intentionally humanize their communication. They reach out proactively, offer personalized feedback, and take time to understand each student's unique context. For example:

- A brief check-in message to a student who has missed a few deadlines can convey care and concern, rather than judgment.
- Personalized welcome videos, audio feedback, or voice memos can make the virtual experience more intimate and relational.

- Using student names consistently in responses and forums fosters recognition and respect.

These small acts of service, rooted in attentiveness, create a relational presence that compensates for physical distance and helps students feel seen and valued.

2. Empowering Autonomy and Self-Direction

Online learners often choose this modality for its flexibility, which accommodates diverse life circumstances, including full-time jobs, caregiving responsibilities, and geographical constraints. However, this flexibility requires a corresponding level of self-regulation, time management, and intrinsic motivation. Not all students arrive with these skills fully developed.

Here again, servant leadership provides a robust framework. Rather than enforcing compliance through rigid rules or punitive consequences, servant leaders support students in developing the capacities needed for independent learning. They do so by:

- Encouraging metacognitive practices, such as reflection journals or goal-setting activities.
- Designing scaffolded assignments that gradually increase in complexity and autonomy.

- Providing clear, compassionate guidance while allowing room for student voice and choice.

Faculty can also model leadership by example, sharing their own experiences with persistence, resilience, and personal growth. In group work or discussion forums, students can be invited to take on leadership roles, facilitating conversations, offering peer feedback, or curating resources. These opportunities help cultivate ownership, confidence, and a growth mindset.

3. Designing Values-Driven, Student-Centered Learning Environments

Online education allows for creative and flexible course design, unconstrained by the time and space limitations of face-to-face instruction. This flexibility makes it possible to embed servant leadership principles directly into the curriculum and learning experience.

A servant-led course is not merely one that teaches about leadership—it practices leadership as pedagogy. For example:

- Discussion forums can be structured to promote empathy and active listening, with prompts that ask students to reflect on lived experiences or explore ethical dimensions of course content.

- Peer-to-peer activities, such as collaborative projects or peer assessments, can foster mutual responsibility and community-building.
- Service-learning components or real-world problem-solving assignments can extend the spirit of service beyond the classroom into students' communities.

Importantly, servant leadership also entails responsiveness to diversity and inclusion. Online students come from varied racial, cultural, linguistic, and socio-economic backgrounds. They may also face accessibility barriers or learning differences. A servant leader designs with these realities in mind, using universal design principles, inclusive language, and culturally responsive pedagogy. They solicit feedback, adapt when needed, and advocate for equity at the institutional level.

4. Leveraging Asynchronous Communication as a Tool for Intentional Connection

The asynchronous nature of many online courses—where students and faculty engage with content at different times—can be seen as a limitation. However, from a servant leadership perspective, it offers a unique opportunity for thoughtful, intentional communication.

In contrast to spontaneous, real-time conversations, asynchronous interactions can be crafted with care. Faculty have time to reflect before responding, to choose words that uplift and encourage, and to create messaging that aligns with servant leadership values. For example:

- An announcement reminding students of an upcoming assignment can include affirmations of their effort and acknowledgement of competing demands.
- Feedback on a paper can highlight not only what needs improvement, but what shows promise—guiding the student's growth with respect and insight.
- A video message at midterm can express appreciation for student engagement and invite suggestions for improving the course experience.

When approached intentionally, these moments become acts of service, reinforcing the faculty member's presence, reliability, and moral leadership.

5. Faculty Autonomy and Non-Hierarchical Structures

Another reason servant leadership aligns so well with online education is that many online programs have decentralized structures. Faculty often operate with significant autonomy, especially in adjunct or part-time roles, and may not be physically embedded within departmental hierarchies. This structure mirrors the non-hierarchical ethos of servant leadership, where leadership is not about rank, but about relational influence and ethical example.

Online faculty are frequently the primary point of contact for students. This proximity gives them a unique opportunity to act as frontline servant leaders—building relationships, modeling integrity, and advocating for student needs. They may not always hold formal leadership positions, but their influence is no less significant. As role models, mentors, and guides, online educators shape the learning climate in powerful and lasting ways.

6. Supporting Student Retention, Success, and Equity

Ultimately, the impact of servant leadership in online higher education is not just theoretical—it is empirical. A growing body of research indicates that student retention and satisfaction are closely tied to relational factors such as perceived instructor presence, responsiveness, and respect.

Students who feel supported, valued, and understood are more likely to:

- Persist through challenges
- Engage more deeply with course material
- Collaborate constructively with peers

- Seek help when needed
- Believe in their own capacity for success

For historically underserved students—first-generation learners, students of color, adult learners, and those with disabilities—the relational and inclusive nature of servant leadership can help close opportunity gaps and reduce feelings of alienation. It provides a foundation for belonging, resilience, and hope, which are crucial for thriving in the often-impersonal world of online education.

Online higher education is not simply a digital version of traditional instruction—it is a distinct educational ecosystem, with its own rhythms, constraints, and possibilities. In this context, servant leadership is not just relevant—it is revolutionary.

By placing care, empathy, and service at the heart of teaching, faculty can transform virtual classrooms into communities of growth. They can foster not only academic success, but also personal development, ethical reflection, and a deep sense of connection—qualities that will shape students not just as learners, but as leaders in their own right.

But at its heart, servant leadership begins with a choice: to lead with humility, intention, and a commitment to the flourishing of others.

Contemporary Applications in Virtual Organizations and Education

The 21st century has witnessed a profound transformation in the way organizations operate and deliver value. Fueled by rapid advances in technology, globalization, and shifting workforce expectations, a growing number of organizations are now entirely virtual or operate in hybrid formats, where remote engagement is central to daily operations. Online educational institutions, remote teams, digital nonprofits, and even telehealth providers are just a few examples of this growing ecosystem.

In these digitally mediated environments, traditional models of leadership—often reliant on proximity, hierarchy, and visible control—become insufficient. Without the physical cues, command structures, or immediate oversight that have historically defined leadership, a new model is required—one that fosters trust, empowers individuals, and sustains human connection across distances. Servant leadership offers precisely this model.

The Rise of Virtual Organizations: New Needs, New Norms

Virtual organizations are inherently decentralized. Whether in education, business, or nonprofit sectors, they operate across time zones, cultures, and technological platforms. This decentralization presents both opportunities and challenges.

On one hand, virtual environments allow for flexibility, diversity, and global reach. On the other, they can breed isolation, miscommunication, and disengagement if not managed with care and intentionality.

Leadership in these settings demands a high degree of emotional intelligence, empathy, and relational acumen—qualities that servant leadership not only values but actively cultivates. Unlike authoritative models that rely on visibility and control, servant leadership thrives in environments where leaders must earn trust rather than assume it, and where influence flows from character and care, not title or tenure.

Servant Leadership in Online Education: A Model for the Future

Online education exemplifies the need for servant leadership in virtual contexts. From fully online degree programs to professional development webinars, the digital classroom is now a dominant learning platform.

Faculty operating in these environments face a set of unique responsibilities:

- Facilitating engagement without the benefit of physical presence.

- Supporting learners with widely varying schedules, technological access, and life circumstances.
- Designing meaningful, inclusive, and flexible learning experiences.

Servant leadership offers a roadmap for addressing these responsibilities with intention and humanity.

Practical Applications in Online Teaching

Instructors who adopt a servant leadership approach in the virtual classroom embody its principles in both design and delivery. Examples include:

- **Student-centered course design:** Servant leaders understand that learning is not a one-size-fits-all experience. They design courses with flexibility and autonomy in mind, offering students choices in assignments, pacing, and collaborative formats. A project-based course might allow students to choose topics relevant to their personal or professional lives, thereby making learning more meaningful and empowering.

- **Flexible communication practices:** Recognizing the complexity of students' lives, faculty can maintain flexible office hours, offer asynchronous engagement options, and respond to student inquiries in a timely, respectful manner. This signals availability and respect, reducing the power differential that can exist in more rigid learning models.

- **Cultivation of online learning communities:** Servant leadership emphasizes belonging. Faculty can use tools like discussion boards, social media groups, or community check-ins to create a sense of camaraderie. Facilitating peer-to-peer dialogue and collaborative assignments nurtures mutual support and shared responsibility for learning.

- **Student voice and feedback integration:** Courses should evolve with students. Servant leaders invite feedback not just at the end of a term, but throughout the learning journey. Implementing changes based on student input reinforces the message that their experiences and insights are valued.

- **Mentorship beyond the classroom:** Servant leadership extends beyond content delivery. Faculty can mentor students through career guidance, research opportunities, or leadership development. Writing letters of recommendation, connecting students to professional networks, or offering coaching sessions reinforces the long-term investment in students' growth.

Faculty Development Through Servant Leadership

Institutions are increasingly embedding servant leadership into faculty development programs, recognizing that ethical and relational teaching practices are essential in virtual learning. These development efforts often focus on:

- **Reflective practice:** Encouraging faculty to examine their own motivations, values, and assumptions about power, authority, and service in teaching.

- **Ethical pedagogy:** Emphasizing inclusivity, accessibility, and integrity in course design and instruction.

- **Peer learning communities:** Creating spaces where faculty can share challenges, strategies, and support, modeling the community-building they aim to foster with students.

Programs that cultivate these competencies help create a culture of leadership at every level, where each faculty member serves as a model of compassion, equity, and lifelong learning.

Servant Leadership in Virtual Organizational Culture

Beyond the classroom, entire virtual institutions and organizations can adopt servant leadership as a foundational philosophy. This involves rethinking the very structure and ethos of the organization.

Institutional Characteristics of Servant-Led Virtual Organizations

- **Flattened hierarchies:** Servant-led institutions reduce bureaucratic layers to empower teams and individuals. Leaders view themselves as facilitators and enablers, not gatekeepers. For example, involving faculty and students in curriculum governance fosters ownership and shared responsibility.

- **Transparent decision-making:** Regular, open communication about institutional goals, policy changes, and resource allocation fosters trust. When leaders admit mistakes, share learning, and seek input, it signals humility and authenticity—hallmarks of servant leadership.

- **Investment in people:** Servant-led institutions prioritize the well-being and development of all members. This includes offering mental health support, equitable compensation, professional growth opportunities, and recognition for contributions.

- **Technology as a servant, not a master:** In virtual settings, technology is central—but in servant leadership models, it is always **in service of human connection and flourishing.** Tools are chosen and implemented with accessibility, inclusivity, and empowerment in mind.

Cross-Sector Applications: Beyond Education

The influence of servant leadership extends well beyond academia. In remote business environments, servant leaders are emerging as effective stewards of organizational culture and performance. Tech companies with distributed teams, such as Basecamp and Buffer, emphasize transparency, mental health, and employee autonomy—practices rooted in servant leadership.

In healthcare, particularly in telehealth environments, the need for empathy, listening, and patient empowerment mirrors the competencies of servant leadership. Digital patient care requires providers to build trust without physical presence—a dynamic similar to online education.

Nonprofits and advocacy organizations, many of which now operate across global virtual networks, also adopt servant leadership to maintain mission integrity, stakeholder inclusion, and team resilience. Their leaders must foster motivation and commitment without the leverage of high salaries or traditional perks. Service, purpose, and integrity become the binding elements.

Why Servant Leadership is Not Just Useful—But Essential

The shift to virtual engagement is not temporary. It represents a permanent reconfiguration of how we work, learn, and lead. In this new normal, servant leadership is not merely relevant—it is increasingly indispensable.

Without the physical and hierarchical structures that once sustained traditional leadership, virtual organizations must lead through influence, not imposition; empathy, not ego. Servant leadership answers this call by re-centering leadership on what matters most: the growth, well-being, and flourishing of people.

Leaders in online education have a particular opportunity—and responsibility—to model this approach. By teaching, guiding, and building communities with intention and care, they prepare students not just for academic success, but for ethical leadership in their own lives and careers.

As organizations continue to evolve in a digital-first world, servant leadership provides a moral and practical compass. Its principles of empathy, empowerment, and stewardship are ideally suited for the fluid, decentralized, and human-centered realities of virtual work and learning.

Online educators and virtual leaders are at the forefront of this transformation. By embracing servant leadership, they demonstrate that compassion and connection are not diminished by distance—they are magnified by it. In doing so, they help create a more just, inclusive, and thriving digital society.

Chapter 2: Servant Leadership in Online Higher Education

The rise of online education, especially in asynchronous formats, has brought profound changes to the structure, delivery, and philosophy of higher learning.

The Role of Faculty as Servant Leaders in Asynchronous Environments

Unlike traditional brick-and-mortar classrooms with fixed schedules and real-time interaction, asynchronous learning provides learners with the freedom to engage at their own pace, on their own time. While this flexibility is one of its greatest strengths, it also poses unique pedagogical and relational challenges. In this evolving academic landscape, faculty members are called not just to teach, but to lead in ways that are empathetic, inclusive, and transformational. This is where the servant leadership model emerges as not only relevant, but essential.

In asynchronous learning environments, faculty no longer serve merely as content transmitters or authority figures. They must operate as facilitators, guides, mentors, and above all, servant leaders.

The core philosophy of servant leadership—put forth by Robert K. Greenleaf—revolves around placing the needs of others first, promoting their growth, and fostering a sense of community and purpose. In the context of online education, this approach aligns beautifully with the demands and opportunities of asynchronous teaching. It reorients the faculty role from one of control to one of care, from one of direction to one of development, and from one of authority to one of authentic presence.

The Need for Human-Centered Leadership in Asynchronous Learning

Asynchronous learning removes temporal and physical constraints, offering unprecedented accessibility to students balancing work, family, health, or geographic limitations. However, the absence of real-time interaction can also create emotional distance, disengagement, and a lack of accountability. Students may feel isolated or unmotivated, unsure whether anyone notices their efforts—or their silence.

Servant-leader faculty recognize these emotional and psychological dynamics. They strive to counterbalance the potentially impersonal nature of asynchronous delivery by fostering relational depth and community presence. Their leadership is not rooted in formal authority, but in their attentiveness to students' experiences and their commitment to holistic student development.

Trust and Presence Without Synchronous Contact

Trust is fundamental in any educational relationship, and it becomes even more critical when the usual cues of eye contact, tone of voice, and body language are missing. Servant leaders in asynchronous classrooms build trust through consistency, transparency, responsiveness, and care.

They establish and maintain a strong presence through:

- Regular, thoughtful announcements that provide updates, encouragement, and context for learning.
- Timely, personalized feedback that affirms effort and guides improvement.
- Active engagement in discussion boards, not to dominate but to enrich and validate student discourse.

- Proactive outreach to students who are falling behind or who haven't participated, signaling attentiveness and concern.

Even without real-time conversation, students come to feel that they are seen, heard, and valued—hallmarks of an effective servant-leader presence.

The Faculty as Relationship Builder and Community Architect

One of the defining responsibilities of servant-leader faculty in asynchronous learning is the intentional creation of community. Virtual classrooms can be perceived as sterile or disconnected unless active efforts are made to humanize them.

Effective strategies include:

- Sharing instructor narratives or reflective prompts, helping students understand the person behind the screen and encouraging reciprocal openness.
- Inviting students to introduce themselves meaningfully, not just with demographics but with their goals, values, or passions.

- Creating collaborative assignments or peer-review activities that require students to learn with and from one another.

- Facilitating community check-ins or gratitude journals, fostering emotional connection and shared reflection.

By investing in these relational dimensions, servant-leader faculty create a space where learners feel they belong—not just academically, but socially and emotionally.

Empowering Student Agency and Autonomy

Asynchronous education is uniquely suited to student-centered learning. Without a rigid schedule or synchronous instruction, students must take initiative in navigating content, deadlines, and collaboration. This reality can be overwhelming—but it is also an opportunity for empowerment.

Servant-leader faculty recognize that one of their central responsibilities is to develop students as autonomous thinkers and leaders. This means:

- Offering assignment choices, allowing students to pursue topics that resonate with their interests and career goals.

- Encouraging peer teaching and leadership, such as assigning rotating discussion moderators or student-led webinars.

- Promoting self-reflection through journals or learning portfolios, enabling students to track their growth and articulate their learning process.

- Framing challenges not as failures, but as learning opportunities, where effort and resilience are valued.

Such practices are aligned with Greenleaf's vision of servant leadership: empowering others so that they too may become leaders in their own right.

Compassionate Policies and Inclusive Practices

Another critical dimension of servant leadership in asynchronous teaching is the institutionalization of compassion through course policies and structures. While fairness and academic rigor remain vital, servant-leader faculty recognize that equity often requires flexibility and contextual judgment.

They may adopt policies that:

- Allow for grace periods or revision opportunities, especially when students face documented hardships.

- Provide multiple means of demonstrating understanding, including videos, infographics, essays, or creative projects.
- Use inclusive language that respects diverse identities and lived experiences.
- Incorporate accessibility tools like closed captions, screen reader-friendly documents, and mobile-friendly layouts.

These practices ensure that no student is left behind due to circumstances unrelated to their intellectual capacity. Servant-leader faculty understand that compassion is not a detour from academic excellence—it is a pathway to it.

Modeling Leadership Through Humility, Purpose, and Growth

Servant leadership also involves modeling core values—humility, resilience, ethical commitment, and purpose. Faculty serve not only as instructors but as examples of how to lead, learn, and live with integrity.

In asynchronous environments, faculty can:

- Share personal learning journeys, including failures and how they overcame them.

- Explicitly connect course content to real-world issues or ethical challenges, inviting students to consider how their learning impacts others.

- Invite constructive feedback from students on the course experience and respond with visible change.

- Reflect on their own teaching practices in weekly messages or forums, modeling lifelong learning and adaptability.

In doing so, they not only teach content—they teach character.

Transforming the Virtual Classroom into a Community of Purpose

Ultimately, servant-leader faculty in asynchronous education are stewards of a learning ecosystem. They do not impose knowledge—they co-create a community where inquiry, care, and curiosity thrive. They leverage the unique affordances of asynchronous learning—not to minimize effort, but to maximize depth, reflection, and inclusivity.

Rather than seeing distance as a barrier, they see it as a canvas—a place where connection must be painted intentionally, with empathy and creativity. Their leadership is quiet, consistent, and powerful. They lead by serving, and in doing so, transform both students and themselves.

Asynchronous online education is not a temporary trend—it is a cornerstone of modern higher education. As more learners turn to virtual platforms for flexibility, access, and opportunity, the role of faculty must evolve accordingly.

Servant leadership offers not just a theoretical framework but a practical blueprint for meeting this moment. By focusing on relationships, empowerment, inclusivity, and moral purpose, servant-leader faculty create learning environments that are both effective and transformative.

In a world increasingly defined by digital interaction and emotional distance, servant leadership reminds us that care is the most powerful tool a teacher can offer. In the hands of faculty who embrace this role, even the most asynchronous classroom can become a place of connection, growth, and lasting impact.

Servant Leadership Through Course Design, LMS Presence, and Communication

Servant leadership in asynchronous online education is not confined to interpersonal interactions or private messaging.

How Digital Design Choices and Engagement Reflect a Deeper Leadership Ethic in Online Higher Education

It is intricately woven into the *very fabric* of the virtual classroom—visible in course architecture, the learning management system (LMS), and every point of communication. For faculty adopting a servant-leader approach, these elements become tools for empowerment, inclusion, and relationship-building.

In a digital space where students may never see their professor in person—or even in real time—the way a course is *designed, maintained, and communicated* becomes the most powerful expression of care and leadership. Every structural choice becomes a reflection of intention. Every announcement becomes a moment of presence. Every feedback comment becomes a formative interaction between mentor and learner.

Let's explore how servant leadership manifests through three interrelated channels: **course design, LMS presence, and communication**—and how these areas together can redefine the student experience in asynchronous higher education.

Course Design as Leadership: Structure as Service

The course shell is typically the first interface students encounter, even before the first message from the instructor. It is a silent messenger, speaking volumes about the instructor's priorities, organization, and regard for the student experience. A poorly designed or cluttered course may inadvertently communicate chaos, indifference, or a lack of care. In contrast, a thoughtfully structured, inclusive course suggests respect, foresight, and commitment to student success—traits that sit at the heart of servant leadership.

Designing with Empathy and Intention

Servant leaders approach course design as a service to learners. They ask questions like:

- *What might confuse or frustrate a first-time student?*
- *How can I build a path that fosters autonomy while reducing unnecessary stress?*
- *What accessibility needs must be met to ensure no student is excluded?*

Their goal is not only clarity but **dignity**. Students should feel that their time, cognitive bandwidth, and diverse backgrounds are honored.

Core strategies include:

- **Logical, minimalist navigation:** Avoiding overly complex module structures or deeply nested folders helps reduce cognitive load.
- **Consistent weekly structure:** Keeping a recognizable rhythm to how each week is presented (e.g., overview,

objectives, content, discussion, assignment) helps students plan and develop habits.

- **Inclusive design features:** Applying **Universal Design for Learning (UDL)** principles ensures all students—regardless of disability, learning style, or cultural background—can engage fully. This includes captioned videos, readable fonts, color contrast, mobile accessibility, and screen-reader compatible documents.

- **Scaffolded assignments:** Breaking major assessments into smaller, manageable parts reduces anxiety and helps students stay on track.

- **Choice and personalization:** Offering options (e.g., select one of three final paper topics, or submit a podcast instead of a paper) supports student agency and different learning preferences.

Community Embedded in Design

A hallmark of servant leadership is building community—and this too can be integrated into course design. Examples include:

- **Introductory discussion boards** that invite students to share not just names and majors, but *values*, goals, and cultural stories.

- **Peer-based learning tasks** like collaborative wikis, group projects, or student-led discussions that foster interdependence.

- **Reflection journals** or multimedia portfolios that connect academic content to personal growth, allowing students to be seen as whole people.

These decisions are more than pedagogical tools—they are *leadership acts*. They signal to students: *You belong here. You matter here.*

LMS Presence as a Servant-Leader Strategy

In asynchronous courses, the LMS (e.g., Canvas, Blackboard, Moodle) functions as the classroom, the bulletin board, the office door, and the coffee shop—all in one. It is where servant-leader faculty "show up" through their digital behavior. This is where presence becomes **felt** rather than **seen**.

Consistency, Rhythm, and Digital Visibility

A servant leader's presence in the LMS is marked by **predictability, warmth, and responsiveness**. While they may not be available 24/7, they create structured rhythms that offer both support and freedom. For example:

- **Weekly announcements** that not only introduce the week's learning goals, but also offer motivational context, relevant current events, or inspirational messages.

- **Timely grading and feedback**—ideally within 3-5 days—so students don't feel their work is disappearing into a void.

- **Midweek check-ins** to remind, re-energize, or course-correct.

- **End-of-week reflections** that help synthesize the learning journey and point toward next steps.

Multimodal Engagement for Human Connection

To bridge the emotional distance of asynchronous interaction, servant leaders often **embed their voice and face** through short videos, audio messages, or narrated presentations. These simple additions help humanize the course and deepen the relational dynamic. Hearing a professor's voice saying, "You're doing great—keep pushing," can carry far more weight than a typed line on a screen.

Other practices include:

- **Video walkthroughs of assignments** to clarify expectations and reduce confusion.

- **LMS-based celebrations** (e.g., "Shout out to Jada for her excellent contribution in this week's thread!") that affirm student achievements.

- **Drop-in feedback spaces** where students can ask questions or seek help outside of private emails, creating a visible community of inquiry.

Humility and Adaptability in the LMS

Servant leaders also model **humility** in how they use the LMS. They invite feedback on course structure, acknowledge when something isn't working, and make visible changes. An anonymous mid-course survey, for instance, invites students into a co-creative process—reminding them they are partners, not just recipients.

Communication as a Servant-Leader Tool

In the absence of face-to-face interaction, **communication becomes the primary currency of leadership.** Every announcement, forum post, email, and grading comment shapes the tone, culture, and emotional experience of the course. Servant leaders do not treat communication as transactional—they treat it as transformational.

Tone as a Mirror of Leadership Values

Tone is especially critical in written communication, where nuance is often lost. Servant leaders strive for a tone that is:

- Warm but professional
- Empathetic yet clear
- Encouraging without being patronizing

They avoid language that implies superiority or detachment. For instance, instead of saying, *"Late work will not be tolerated,"* a servant-leader might write, *"If you're experiencing difficulty meeting a deadline, please reach out—your learning matters, and we'll find a solution together."*

Feedback as Dialogue, Not Verdict

Grading and feedback offer some of the most potent leadership moments. Rather than merely correcting errors, servant leaders:

- Acknowledge effort and growth
- Highlight strengths before discussing weaknesses
- Use a coaching voice, offering guidance and encouragement for the next step
- Provide **actionable next steps**, not vague generalities (e.g., "To deepen this argument, consider incorporating a counterpoint from X author.")

This type of communication is *relational* rather than *judgmental*—it builds trust and a sense of safety in the learning process.

Transparency and Availability

Servant-leader faculty do not pretend to be infallible. They communicate transparently about:

- Course changes or technical issues
- Their own limitations or evolving teaching practices
- Student progress, both individual and class-wide

They also set **clear communication boundaries**—but within those, they are responsive. For example, committing to respond to emails within 24-48 hours, and using auto-responders or LMS messages to communicate delays, helps students feel respected and reduces anxiety.

Communication as Vision Casting

Servant leaders use communication to build not just connection—but *vision*. They help students see how the course ties into:

- Their **personal development**
- Their **career pathways**
- The **greater good** of society

They ask reflective questions like, *"How does this learning impact your future role as a leader or changemaker?"* and frame content around ethical, real-world applications.

The Integrated Impact of Servant Leadership Online

When practiced through course design, LMS presence, and communication, servant leadership is not an abstract philosophy—it becomes a daily practice. It creates an ecosystem where:

- Students feel safe to take intellectual risks.
- Learning is personalized and purposeful.
- Trust replaces surveillance.
- Leadership is modeled, not just discussed.

Servant leaders in asynchronous education recognize that students may never walk into their office, shake their hand, or raise their hand in class. But they **can** still feel seen. They **can** still be challenged to grow. And they **can** still emerge from the course more confident, capable, and connected than when they entered.

These faculty redefine what online teaching can be—not just a platform for information exchange, but a **transformative community** shaped by empathy, empowerment, and purpose.

Humanizing Online Learning:

Humanizing online learning is a central and transformative goal for faculty who embrace the principles of servant leadership. In asynchronous, screen-mediated environments—where there are no hallways to walk down, no spontaneous classroom conversations, and no visible body language—the risk of students feeling unseen, isolated, or detached increases exponentially. Servant leaders recognize this risk and actively work against it. They do not view online teaching as a technical task to be completed, but as a human relationship to be nurtured.

At the core of humanizing education is the conviction that every student matters—not just as an academic performer, but as a *whole person* with a story, emotions, goals, and challenges. Servant-leader educators design online experiences that affirm students' dignity, strengthen connection, and build a relational bridge across the digital divide.

Understanding Students as Individuals

The servant leadership approach begins with *empathy*. Servant-leader faculty are intentional about getting to know their students beyond the metrics of discussion posts and assignment grades. They recognize that every learner enters the online classroom carrying a unique context: full-time jobs, caregiving responsibilities, health conditions, economic pressures, and a variety of cultural or linguistic backgrounds.

To bridge this understanding gap, servant-leader instructors often:

- Use **introductory surveys** to learn about students' learning preferences, challenges, and goals.

- Launch **welcome discussion forums** where students can introduce themselves—not just with a name and major, but with their aspirations, values, or stories.

- Send **check-in messages** during key points in the semester to ask: *"How are you doing—really?"*

- Acknowledge student life events such as illness, job changes, or family obligations with compassion and flexibility.

This effort to understand students as individuals goes beyond courtesy. It's a form of leadership that says: *"I see you. I hear you. I want to support your success, not just evaluate your performance."*

Establishing Instructor Presence in Online Learning

In face-to-face settings, presence happens organically— through smiles, tone of voice, body language, and spontaneous interactions. Online, however, **presence must be engineered** deliberately. It becomes a conscious design and communication strategy, not a passive occurrence. Servant leaders understand that presence is not about being online all the time, but about *being felt*—emotionally, cognitively, and socially.

Ways to Establish Presence:

1. **Personalized Communication**
    - Use students' names regularly in discussions and feedback.
    - Reference specific ideas students have shared to validate their contributions.
    - Reply to inquiries with care, showing attentiveness to the student's concern rather than offering generic responses.

2. **Timely, Relational Feedback**
    - Offer not only grades, but thoughtful comments that coach and affirm.
    - Let students know when they've made progress or taken intellectual risks.
    - Respond to confusion with patience and encouragement, not frustration.

3. **Multimodal Engagement**
    - Incorporate short video or audio messages to introduce modules or provide feedback.
    - Share behind-the-scenes glimpses into the instructor's process or reflections—such as explaining *why* a certain reading was selected or *how* it connects to real-world practice.
    - Use storytelling to bring warmth and narrative depth into the content.

4. **Consistent Rhythm**
    - Establish a reliable schedule for announcements, feedback, and presence.
    - Avoid sudden silences or delays that leave students wondering if their instructor is still "there."

Instructor presence humanizes the learning process by restoring the relational dimension often lost in asynchronous delivery. When students feel their instructor is *with* them—cheering them on, guiding them through struggle—they are more motivated, more likely to persist, and more willing to engage deeply with course content.

Creating a Culture of Compassionate Communication

Language matters—especially in online courses, where tone can be easily misunderstood. Servant-leader faculty adopt a **compassionate and inclusive tone** in all communications. They avoid authoritarian or overly bureaucratic language that may feel impersonal or intimidating.

Compassionate tone involves:

- Greeting students warmly.
- Expressing gratitude for participation and effort.
- Framing errors or missed expectations as learning opportunities, not failures.
- Being clear and firm about expectations, but always with kindness and a solutions-focused approach.

For example, instead of writing, *"You failed to submit the assignment on time,"* a servant leader might say, *"I noticed the assignment wasn't submitted—if something came up, let me know. I'm here to support your progress."*

This style of communication reinforces safety, dignity, and respect—key ingredients in a humanized learning experience.

Fostering Peer-to-Peer Community

While instructor presence is essential, **peer connection** is equally vital for humanizing the online classroom. Students often learn just as much from their classmates as from their instructors. Servant-leader faculty *design for community*, not just content delivery.

They create opportunities for students to:

- Share personal stories or lived experiences as part of content discussions.
- Collaborate on group projects that promote interdependence and mutual respect.
- Reflect on how course content applies to their identities, cultures, and goals.
- Respond to each other in meaningful, affirming ways— moving beyond the "I agree" response to offer genuine engagement.

Community-building design choices include:

- Icebreaker assignments that go beyond basic introductions.
- Structured discussion forums with prompts that invite vulnerability or personal insight.
- Peer feedback assignments where students review each other's work in a supportive, constructive environment.

- Group norms and netiquette guidelines that encourage respectful discourse and inclusion.

Modeling Inclusivity and Ethical Leadership

Servant-leader faculty model the very values they wish to cultivate in students. This includes:

- Welcoming and validating diverse viewpoints.
- Interrupting bias or harmful language in discussions with tact and firmness.
- Centering voices from underrepresented groups in the curriculum.
- Reflecting critically on their own teaching practices and inviting student input for improvement.

They do not simply set the tone—they **are** the tone. By modeling empathy, curiosity, and courage, they empower students to do the same with one another.

Small Gestures, Big Impact

Humanizing learning is not about increasing workload—it is about increasing **intention**. Many of the most powerful humanizing actions are **small but meaningful**:

- A quick video message to congratulate the class after midterms.

- A personalized message to a struggling student offering support.

- Sharing a moment of vulnerability or failure from one's own academic journey.

- Mentioning a student's improvement in a discussion post for the whole class to see.

These acts remind students that behind the screen is a real person who cares deeply about their growth—not just a grader or administrator.

The Payoff: Belonging, Resilience, and Success

When students feel humanized in an online course, several powerful outcomes emerge:

- **Increased engagement:** Students are more likely to participate actively and take intellectual risks.

- **Greater retention:** Students who feel connected to their instructor and peers are less likely to drop out.

- **Higher achievement:** Emotional safety supports cognitive performance.

- **Stronger ethical development:** Students who experience servant leadership are more likely to adopt those values in their own careers.

In short, humanizing online learning does not just make the digital classroom more pleasant—it makes it more powerful.

Humanizing online learning is not a luxury—it is a necessity for creating equitable, engaging, and empowering educational experiences in the digital age. Servant-leader faculty understand this and act accordingly. They weave empathy, presence, and community into every aspect of their teaching practice—not through grand gestures, but through **purposeful, relational design**.

In doing so, they help students feel not only educated but *seen*, not only instructed but *inspired*, and not only included but *valued*. That is the essence of humanizing education—and the lasting legacy of servant leadership online.

Examples of Servant Leadership Behaviors in Online Classrooms

Bringing servant leadership into the virtual classroom is not an abstract ideal—it is a practical, deliberate set of behaviors that manifest daily in the way instructors engage, support, and inspire students. The essence of servant leadership lies in putting the needs of learners first, empowering them to grow not only academically, but also personally and professionally. In online environments—where disconnection and anonymity can easily take hold—these behaviors become even more essential.

Below are several key examples of servant leadership behaviors in online classrooms. These actions demonstrate empathy, reinforce student dignity, promote growth, and foster a strong, inclusive learning community. When implemented consistently, these behaviors transform online courses from transactional experiences into meaningful human connections that fuel learning and development.

1. Thoughtful Feedback as a Vehicle for Growth

Feedback is more than a grading function; it is one of the most significant tools an instructor has to influence student learning, motivation, and confidence. In a servant leadership framework, feedback is relational. It is not merely a summative judgment of right or wrong but a formative, dialogic interaction aimed at helping the student grow.

Characteristics of Thoughtful Feedback in a Servant-Leadership Approach:

- **Personalization:** Servant-leader faculty engage directly with students' ideas. They reference specific phrases, arguments, or creative choices the student made, showing that their work was read carefully and with respect. This fosters a sense of personal investment and validation.

Example: "I noticed the way you connected the concept of cognitive dissonance to your own experience in marketing—that's a powerful and insightful application."

- **Constructive, Respectful Language:** The tone of feedback matters just as much as the content. Servant leaders frame critiques as opportunities for improvement, not as expressions of disappointment or frustration. They provide actionable suggestions while maintaining a tone of care and belief in the student's capacity to improve.

Example: "Your argument has a strong foundation. To make it even more persuasive, consider providing one more real-world example that aligns with your thesis."

- **Encouragement and Acknowledgment:** Every piece of feedback contains an opportunity to affirm effort, creativity, or progress. By acknowledging what students did well, instructors reinforce positive behaviors and boost motivation.

Example: "You've really grown in your ability to synthesize multiple sources this term—it's exciting to see your development."

- **Timeliness:** Servant leaders understand that delayed feedback can hinder learning. They commit to turnaround times that allow students to reflect, adjust, and apply insights in upcoming assignments. Timely responses also demonstrate respect for the student's investment in their education.

By offering feedback that is respectful, formative, and grounded in empathy, servant-leader faculty reinforce their commitment to the development of the whole student—not just academic performance, but confidence and voice.

2. Responsiveness and Availability: Building Trust Through Consistency

In online courses, where asynchronous learning is common, students often feel uncertain about when or if they'll hear back from instructors. This uncertainty can lead to anxiety, disengagement, and a perception of indifference. Servant leaders proactively counter this dynamic by ensuring their presence is both felt and accessible.

Practices that Reflect Responsiveness:

- **Clear Communication Policies:** Servant leaders set transparent expectations for communication early in the course. They specify their average response times (e.g., within 24-48 hours), provide preferred contact methods, and encourage students to reach out when needed. This clarity builds a sense of reliability and structure.

- **Regular Check-Ins:** Weekly messages, reflection prompts, or informal surveys help maintain connection and momentum. These check-ins do not have to be lengthy—they simply need to remind students that the instructor is attuned to their progress and available for support.

Example: A short message like "As we head into Week 5, I'd love to know: what's one thing that's been working well for you in this course so far?" invites dialogue and human connection.

- **Flexible Office Hours:** Servant leaders accommodate students in various time zones and life circumstances by offering flexible virtual meetings. These might include drop-in hours, appointments by request, or rotating availability times to ensure broad access.

- **Emergency Support and Grace:** Life happens, and servant leaders recognize this. When students face illness, family emergencies, or technological setbacks, servant-leader faculty respond with empathy and flexibility. They do not enforce policies rigidly at the expense of humanity.

Availability is not about being online 24/7—it's about being *dependable* and *present* in a way that students can trust. This presence becomes a stabilizing force in the often-uncertain world of remote learning.

3. Community-Oriented Announcements: Leading With Care and Inspiration

In many online courses, the announcements section is underutilized—limited to reminders about deadlines or logistical details. Servant leaders, however, recognize announcements as a leadership platform. They use them to inspire, build morale, and reinforce the relational fabric of the course.

Elements of Effective, Community-Oriented Announcements:

- **Recognition of Student Efforts:** Celebrating individual or collective achievements—such as a high-quality discussion thread, improvement on an assignment, or creative application of course concepts—helps students feel seen and appreciated.

Example: "Shoutout to everyone who contributed to this week's discussion on equity—your responses were thoughtful and challenging in the best way. Special thanks to Marco for bringing in a global perspective."

- **Encouragement and Motivation:** Servant leaders are tuned into the emotional rhythms of a semester. During midterms, holidays, or stressful weeks, they offer words of encouragement to help students persist and focus.

Example: "I know this week is heavy with assignments across your courses—remember to take breaks, hydrate, and reach out if you need support."

- **Contextual Connections:** Making course content relevant to real-world events or professional fields helps students see the value of their learning. Servant leaders draw these connections regularly, showing attentiveness to the world beyond the screen.

- **Reflection Prompts:** Inviting students to reflect on what they're learning or how they're growing fosters metacognition and deepens engagement. Even brief prompts in announcements can plant seeds for powerful introspection.

In using announcements not just to instruct but to connect, servant leaders transform them into moments of shared meaning and motivation.

4. Supporting Personal and Professional Growth: Seeing the Whole Student

True servant leadership looks beyond the course syllabus. It considers students not just as learners, but as emerging professionals, leaders, and citizens. Servant-leader faculty take an active interest in helping students prepare for life beyond the classroom.

Ways Faculty Can Support Broader Growth:

- **Career Guidance and Resources:** This might include sharing internship opportunities, field-specific articles, alumni insights, or tips for building a portfolio. Servant leaders recognize when students express vocational curiosity and help them take the next step.

Example: "If you're interested in pursuing a role in policy analysis, the Brookings Institution just opened applications for their summer research fellowship."

- **Mentorship Opportunities:** Some students benefit greatly from informal mentoring—conversations about goals, encouragement to apply for leadership positions, or simply having someone to offer perspective. Writing letters of recommendation, inviting students to co-present at conferences, or providing feedback on job applications are all acts of service.

- **Leadership Development Within the Course:** Group projects or discussion forums provide opportunities for students to take initiative. Servant-leader instructors recognize and cultivate these moments—encouraging students to moderate a thread, coordinate a team, or contribute ideas for course improvement.

- **Values Integration:** Servant leaders help students connect their learning to their values. They ask questions like, *"How does this concept align with your personal or professional mission?"* or *"How might you apply this theory in your community?"*

Supporting students in this holistic way transforms education from a content-delivery model into a mentorship-driven journey of discovery.

Servant leadership in online education is not about grand gestures or additional workload—it is about *intentional care*. The behaviors described here—thoughtful feedback, consistent availability, culture-building announcements, and whole-person support—are deeply human actions that elevate digital learning into a transformative experience.

Importantly, these behaviors ripple outward. When students experience servant leadership, they often mirror those values in their own interactions—whether in future classrooms, professional settings, or community spaces. They learn that leadership is not about authority or control, but about empathy, collaboration, and service.

By modeling these practices in virtual classrooms, faculty members don't just teach content—they teach a way of being. They cultivate not only smarter students, but wiser, kinder, and more empowered human beings.

And in that, the mission of servant leadership in education finds its greatest success.

This commitment to student growth aligns directly with Greenleaf's principle that servant leaders seek to nurture others into leaders themselves. It transforms education from a transactional process into a transformative experience.

Incorporating these behaviors into online teaching is not about perfection or performative care.

It is about genuine engagement, intentionality, and a commitment to student well-being. Faculty who embody these practices create online environments where learning is not only effective but deeply human. As the digital classroom continues to evolve, servant leadership offers a powerful framework for making it a place of empathy, connection, and lasting impact.

Chapter 3: Modeling Leadership Through Online Course Design and Communication

In online higher education, where face-to-face interaction is often limited or entirely absent, the architecture of the course and the intentionality behind every communication become pivotal. This chapter explores how faculty can model leadership through two key domains: course design and communication.

More specifically, it focuses on designing leadership-infused syllabi and **LMS** (Learning Management System) structures, as well as leveraging course announcements as moments of servant leadership.

By embedding leadership values into these foundational aspects of online teaching, faculty don't just convey information; they set the tone, culture, and moral compass of the virtual classroom.

Servant leadership is not an external supplement to pedagogy—it is the framework upon which impactful teaching and learning rest.

The ability to lead students through empathetic communication, transparent structures, and purpose-driven course elements shapes not only academic outcomes but also the character and aspirations of learners.

Faculty are more than content experts; they are leadership models whose daily interactions teach far more than just disciplinary knowledge.

Designing Leadership-Infused Syllabi and LMS Structures

In the online learning environment, students often encounter two primary points of orientation before any course content is explored: the syllabus and the Learning Management System (LMS).

These elements are not merely logistical tools—they are also powerful cultural artifacts. They frame the learning experience, shape expectations, and convey the values of the instructor and the institution.

When designed with servant leadership principles in mind, both the syllabus and the LMS become active agents in fostering clarity, trust, empowerment, and a sense of shared purpose.

By embedding leadership values into these foundational course structures, educators can create a learning environment that models the very leadership behaviors they seek to instill—thoughtfulness, inclusion, adaptability, and empathy.

The Syllabus as a Leadership Tool

Traditionally, the syllabus has been approached as a contractual document: a static, rule-heavy overview of policies, deadlines, and grading systems. While this functional purpose is important, such an approach often prioritizes control and compliance over connection and curiosity. In contrast, a leadership-infused syllabus reconceives the document as a relational and aspirational tool—a guide that frames the course as a shared journey toward growth.

Key characteristics of a leadership-oriented syllabus include:

1. Inclusive and Supportive Language

Rather than using punitive or formal legalese, leadership-infused syllabi are written in welcoming, empathetic, and student-centered language. Policies are framed as community agreements rather than threats. For instance:

- Instead of: *"Late work will not be accepted without documentation."*
- Use: *"I understand that life can be unpredictable. If you're facing challenges meeting a deadline, please reach out so we can work together on a solution."*

This tone reinforces mutual respect and encourages open communication—an essential trait in effective leadership.

2. Transparent Expectations and Accessible Support

A good syllabus demystifies the course experience. It outlines **learning goals, assignment rubrics, participation criteria, and weekly expectations** with clarity. Transparency reduces ambiguity and stress, which in turn fosters student confidence and autonomy. A well-structured syllabus:

- Details the purpose of each assignment and how it connects to learning outcomes.
- Outlines clear grading criteria with student-friendly language.
- Includes a weekly or modular roadmap to help students plan ahead.

Including support structures—such as links to mental health services, tutoring centers, accessibility offices, and communication channels with the instructor—further reinforces that students are not navigating their journey alone.

3. Empathy and Flexibility

Acknowledging the humanity of students is a foundational element of servant leadership. Leadership-oriented syllabi anticipate life challenges and communicate an openness to adaptation. This might include:

- Policies that allow for grace periods or flexible participation windows.
- A section on "What to do if you're falling behind" with step-by-step instructions for reconnecting.
- Encouragement for students to communicate personal or academic concerns without fear of judgment.

4. Instructor Values and Commitment

Including a **personal welcome message** or a **"Teaching Philosophy"** section adds authenticity and relational depth. Here, the instructor can briefly articulate their commitment to equity, inclusivity, and leadership development. For example:

"In this course, I see each of you not just as students but as emerging professionals and leaders. My goal is to support your growth—academically and personally—by fostering a community where everyone's voice matters and learning is collaborative."

This transparency builds trust and models the kind of value-driven leadership the course encourages.

5. Shared Ownership

Where appropriate, consider **co-creating aspects of the syllabus** with students during the first week of class. This may include:

- Setting community guidelines for respectful communication.
- Allowing students to vote on optional assignment formats.
- Gathering input on topics or case studies that align with their interests or professional goals.

Co-creating elements of the course invites student agency and communicates that leadership is not top-down—it's shared and participatory.

LMS Structure as an Extension of Leadership

While the syllabus introduces the tone and expectations of the course, the **Learning Management System (LMS)** is where students engage with content, interact with peers, and complete most of their learning activities. A **leadership-infused LMS design** functions not just as a content delivery system, but as a **carefully designed ecosystem** that reflects the instructor's priorities: accessibility, clarity, growth, and support.

Core components of a leadership-oriented LMS design include:

1. Consistent and Intuitive Organization

A clear and predictable structure reduces cognitive overload, especially for students balancing work, family, or neurodiverse learning needs. Modules should:

- Follow a consistent format each week (e.g., overview, readings, lecture, discussion, assignment).
- Include clearly labeled folders and files (e.g., "Week 2: Community Health & Equity" rather than "Module 2").
- Minimize unnecessary clutter or hidden links.

This attention to clarity models leadership behaviors such as strategic thinking, organization, and user-centered planning.

2. Student-Centered Navigation

Students should not have to dig to find critical information. A student-first LMS layout might include:

- A **"Start Here"** section with the syllabus, instructor introduction video, FAQ, and technology tour.

- Clearly accessible links to grades, announcements, office hours, and key course materials.

- A **dashboard or checklist** of weekly tasks to promote self-management and accountability.

The LMS becomes a reflection of servant leadership's emphasis on **removing obstacles** and setting others up for success.

3. Embedded Support Resources

Rather than relegating support services to a sidebar or forgotten tab, embed them contextually throughout the course. Examples include:

- Links to the writing center within assignment instructions.

- Video tutorials and help guides in each week's module.

- A dedicated **"Student Support Hub"** within the LMS, featuring mental health resources, time management tools, and peer-to-peer help forums.

This integration reinforces the value of community care and ensures students are reminded, often and visibly, that help is always within reach.

4. Spaces for Reflection and Growth

Leadership development requires reflection. Create structured opportunities for students to think critically about their learning, values, and growth. Possible approaches include:

- A **"Leadership Journal"** with biweekly prompts related to course content and personal insights.

- Optional **"Reflection Corners"** in each module where students respond to questions like, "What challenged your thinking this week?"

- A **Leadership Discussion Board** where students can share how course concepts apply to real-world or professional contexts.

By valuing reflection, the LMS affirms that **learning is both an internal and external journey**—one that calls for self-awareness as much as content mastery.

Both the syllabus and LMS serve as **silent teachers**. Even before an instructor writes their first announcement or gives their first lecture, students are forming impressions about the course, the instructor, and the expectations they will face. When crafted with care and infused with servant leadership values, these tools communicate: *You are capable. You are supported. You are part of something meaningful.*

Leadership in education isn't always about what we say—it's about how we design, respond, and invite students into their own growth. A thoughtful syllabus and an empowering LMS are acts of leadership in themselves. They offer structure without rigidity, clarity without authoritarianism, and support without condescension. Most importantly, they set the stage for a learning environment where students don't just earn grades—they become leaders.

Course Announcements as Leadership Moments

In online learning, course announcements are often the primary mode of ongoing communication. They are tools for coordination and reminders—but they are also powerful vehicles for modeling leadership. Every announcement provides an opportunity to communicate not only logistical details but also values, encouragement, and vision.

Announcements as Relational Anchors

A servant-leader approach to announcements transforms them from mechanical updates into meaningful touchpoints. These messages become weekly moments of connection, alignment, and community-building. Faculty can use announcements to:

- **Express care and empathy:** Acknowledge busy times in the semester, encourage self-care, and offer supportive messages when students may be struggling.

- **Celebrate growth:** Highlight examples of insightful student work or note progress toward course goals.

- **Create transparency:** Share the rationale behind teaching choices or assignment designs to reinforce mutual trust.

- **Reinforce course values:** Tie content to broader themes such as ethics, civic responsibility, or the pursuit of excellence.

These relational anchors help students feel connected and valued, even in the absence of synchronous interaction.

Practical Strategies for Leadership-Infused Announcements

Faculty can adopt several best practices to make their announcements vehicles for servant leadership:

- **Consistency and rhythm:** Send announcements on a regular schedule (e.g., weekly updates on Monday mornings) to establish trust and reliability.

- **Personalization:** Address students directly, refer to ongoing discussions, and use a warm, conversational tone.

- **Use of multimedia:** Include video or audio updates to convey tone and presence more effectively than text alone.

- **Calls to reflection:** Encourage students to consider questions such as, "What leadership lesson did you take from this week's reading?" or "How did you support a peer in this week's discussion?"

- **Modeling vulnerability and growth:** Share stories of your own learning journey, including missteps and insights, to normalize imperfection and model resilience.

Encouraging Student-Led Communication

Servant leadership is not only about how instructors lead; it's also about how they develop leadership in others. One way to do this is by inviting students to take the lead on communication. For example, faculty might:

- Assign rotating student roles to write weekly class summaries or inspirational messages.
- Encourage peer-led discussions with opening prompts.
- Create an "Ask a Peer" thread where students can support one another with technical or content-related questions.

These practices not only reduce instructor workload but also cultivate student agency, ownership, and community.

Modeling leadership in online teaching is a subtle yet powerful endeavor. It requires mindfulness, consistency, and an unwavering commitment to student development. Through thoughtfully designed syllabi, LMS structures, and course announcements, faculty can exemplify servant leadership in action. These elements, though often perceived as administrative or procedural, are actually integral to the moral and pedagogical fabric of the course.

When approached with intention, these tools transcend their logistical functions and become mechanisms for growth, empathy, and empowerment. In this way, faculty do not merely teach leadership; they live it. And in doing so, they shape not only the academic journeys of their students but also the leadership capacity of the next generation.

Board Facilitation Techniques That Build Leadership Values

Discussion boards are foundational components of asynchronous online education. They are more than platforms for course content interaction—they are spaces where students can grow as thinkers, communicators, collaborators, and emerging leaders.

When intentionally designed and facilitated through the lens of **servant leadership**, these boards become developmental arenas for leadership values such as empathy, integrity, respect, collaboration, critical thinking, and self-awareness.

Effective faculty presence on discussion boards requires more than enforcing participation requirements or grading rubrics. Servant-leader educators actively cultivate intellectual and emotional engagement, nurture students' voices, and model constructive, values-driven communication.

The following facilitation techniques provide strategies for using discussion boards as transformative tools for leadership development.

1. Crafting Prompts That Inspire Leadership Thinking

The heart of any meaningful discussion is the **question posed.** Servant-leader faculty design prompts that move students beyond rote memorization or superficial commentary.

Instead, they encourage dialogue that invites introspection, ethical reasoning, and real-world application. Thoughtful prompts challenge students to reflect not just on what they know, but on who they are becoming as learners and leaders.

Examples of leadership-oriented prompts include:

- "Describe a moment when you had to lead or support a team under challenging circumstances. What values guided your actions?"

- "How can the principles discussed in this week's reading be applied to inclusive leadership in your professional field?"

- "Reflect on a recent decision you made. How might servant leadership have influenced that choice differently?"

- "Who in your life exemplifies servant leadership? How do their actions shape your understanding of effective leadership?"

- "Identify a societal or organizational problem. What would a servant-leader approach to solving this issue look like?"

These types of prompts invite students to connect course content to lived experiences, ethical dilemmas, and leadership contexts. They reinforce the idea that leadership is not a title but a practice—one that can be cultivated through reflection, choice, and service to others.

2. Modeling Leadership in Faculty Responses

Faculty participation in discussion boards should model the type of leadership behaviors and communication styles that the course seeks to develop.

A servant-leader faculty member sees their role as facilitator, guide, and coach, not just evaluator. Their responses are grounded in respect, encouragement, and thoughtful **provocation.**

Effective faculty practices include:

- **Asking open-ended follow-up questions** that deepen student thinking or present contrasting viewpoints:

    "You mention the importance of integrity in your leadership approach. How do you balance

transparency with confidentiality in professional settings?"

- **Acknowledging vulnerability and emotional insight** with affirming language:

"Thank you for sharing that personal story—it really highlights how empathy can influence our decisions as leaders."

- **Reframing missteps as growth opportunities:**

"That's an interesting perspective. Let's explore how another leadership framework might challenge or support your view."

- **Highlighting connections between students' responses** to build a sense of shared learning:

"You and James both touched on the idea of accountability. What similarities do you see in your experiences?"

Faculty tone is critical. When instructors model patience, humility, and intellectual curiosity, students internalize these values. They learn that leadership is not about always having the right answer—it's about listening deeply, responding thoughtfully, and engaging ethically.

3. Encouraging Peer Leadership

One of the most impactful strategies in online discussions is inviting students to take ownership of their learning community.

Assigning or encouraging peer facilitation roles can empower students to practice leadership skills in real-time.

Peer leadership strategies include:

- **Rotating discussion facilitators:** Assign students to lead a weekly discussion thread by summarizing key readings, posing questions, and encouraging responses.

- **Thread summarizers:** Appoint a student to synthesize the week's conversation and highlight key themes, insights, or questions that emerged.

- **Response leaders:** Ask certain students to focus on responding to under-engaged posts to ensure that every voice is acknowledged.

- **"Leadership Spotlights":** Have students select a classmate's comment each week to recognize for clarity, insight, or value alignment.

Instructors support peer leadership by:

- Providing clear expectations or templates for facilitation roles.

- Offering constructive feedback on students' facilitation efforts.
- Publicly acknowledging and appreciating leadership contributions.

This distributed model of leadership reinforces the idea that everyone can lead, regardless of formal authority. It also encourages collaboration, builds peer accountability, and cultivates a sense of shared responsibility for the classroom environment.

4. Fostering a Culture of Recognition and Respect

Beyond structured roles, servant-leader faculty cultivate a classroom culture where mutual recognition and gratitude are the norm. Online environments can often feel depersonalized; affirming each other's contributions helps rehumanize the learning experience.

Techniques to foster a respectful and inclusive climate include:

- Encouraging students to respond to at least one peer with a comment that highlights a strength in their post.
- Using built-in platform features like "likes" or "stars" to allow low-stakes, immediate feedback.

- Creating a "Shout-Out Thread" where students can publicly thank or celebrate classmates' insights.
- Modeling respectful disagreement and demonstrating how to engage in civil, productive debate.

By valuing each person's contribution—regardless of style, background, or opinion—servant-leader educators promote psychological safety, a critical component of both learning and leadership development.

5. Balancing Structure and Flexibility

Not all students approach discussion boards with the same level of comfort, confidence, or communicative fluency. Servant leadership in the online classroom means recognizing and adapting to these differences without compromising learning goals.

Ways to support diverse engagement include:

- Allowing multimedia responses (e.g., short video reflections or voice memos) for students who express themselves better verbally.
- Providing alternative prompts or supplemental questions for students who want different entry points into the conversation.

- Offering deadlines with buffers, understanding that life circumstances sometimes interrupt ideal participation.
- Encouraging personal connections to content to honor students' cultural or professional backgrounds.

By honoring different ways of thinking and expressing leadership, faculty help every student see themselves as capable of contribution. Flexibility, in this context, is not a lack of rigor—it is a form of respect and inclusion.

When implemented with intention and care, discussion boards become more than just forums for academic discourse. They evolve into transformative spaces where students practice listening, questioning, reflecting, and leading.

Faculty, as servant leaders, facilitate this transformation by modeling humility, encouraging ownership, and fostering a shared sense of purpose.

Leadership is cultivated in moments of conversation, recognition, and reflection. Online discussions—when skillfully guided—offer these moments in abundance. Through this dialogic space, students not only learn to lead others but begin to better understand themselves. This is the heart of leadership education—and the legacy of a servant-led classroom.

Model Empathy and Active Listening

Online education can suffer from a sense of depersonalization. Text-based communication, while efficient, often lacks the nuance of human tone, facial expression, and body language. Servant-leader faculty counter this challenge by integrating video tools that convey presence, empathy, and responsiveness.

Video feedback and video chats are powerful tools to humanize learning and model servant leadership behaviors, particularly empathy and active listening.

The Power of Video Feedback

Video feedback allows instructors to offer personalized, rich, and emotionally resonant responses to student work. Rather than a few typed comments in the margins, a short video lets students hear the instructor's voice, see their facial expressions, and sense their engagement.

Servant-leader video feedback practices include:

- **Starting with affirmation:** Begin by highlighting the strengths of the student's work and effort.

- **Being present and conversational:** Use a natural, encouraging tone. Speak to the student as a whole person, not just as a name on an assignment.

- **Clarifying suggestions with tone and gesture:** Video allows faculty to soften critiques, show enthusiasm, or pause for reflection—nuances often lost in writing.

- **Closing with encouragement:** Reinforce belief in the student's potential and express excitement about their continued learning.

Video feedback takes time, but even occasional use—especially on major assignments—can significantly enhance student motivation and trust. It demonstrates care and commitment, hallmarks of servant leadership.

Optional Video Chats and Virtual Office Hours

While not all students will be comfortable or available for live interaction, offering optional video chats can be an important form of support. These sessions may include:

- **Virtual office hours:** Provide flexible times for students to drop in with questions, clarifications, or concerns.

- **Individual check-ins:** Offer 10-15 minute one-on-one meetings to connect mid-semester or after major assessments.
- **Small group discussions:** Facilitate deeper engagement and peer bonding in low-pressure formats.

The presence of video chats signals that the instructor is accessible and invested. It provides students with a human connection that text alone may not achieve.

During these sessions, servant-leader faculty model active listening by:

- Making eye contact (through the camera).
- Paraphrasing student concerns to confirm understanding.
- Asking open-ended questions that explore needs and goals.
- Responding with empathy and affirmation.

These practices not only resolve logistical issues but also build trust, reduce anxiety, and deepen students' sense of belonging.

Equity and Accessibility Considerations

As servant leaders, faculty must also be mindful of the barriers that video communication can present. Not all students have the same access to high-speed internet, quiet environments, or comfort with video interaction.

Servant-leader strategies to ensure equity include:

- Always offering alternatives to video (e.g., phone calls, written responses).
- Recording and sharing asynchronous video updates for those who cannot attend live.
- Using captioning and transcripts to support accessibility.
- Being flexible and understanding about student preferences and constraints.

By centering the student experience and prioritizing inclusivity, faculty ensure that video tools enhance, rather than complicate, the learning environment.

In sum, modeling leadership through discussion facilitation and video communication allows faculty to bring servant leadership principles to life in the online classroom. These practices create space for students to explore their values, develop leadership capacities, and connect meaningfully with both peers and instructors.

They also remind students that leadership is not about command and control—it is about presence, empathy, and relational depth. Faculty who lead in these ways do not just teach content; they shape communities and cultivate character. And in doing so, they prepare students to carry servant leadership into their professions, communities, and lives beyond the classroom.

Inclusive, Community-Building Practices in Grading and Feedback

In the servant leadership model, every interaction with students is an opportunity to foster dignity, growth, and inclusion.

Nowhere is this more critical than in the practices of grading and feedback—two areas that significantly influence student motivation, performance, and sense of belonging.

Traditional grading systems often emphasize assessment over development, placing the instructor in a gatekeeping role. Servant leadership reimagines grading as a process of mutual engagement, empowerment, and support. It requires educators to reflect not just on what is being evaluated, but how and why.

Grading for Growth, Not Just Judgment

Servant-leader faculty approach grading with the mindset of stewardship and development. They recognize that grades are not just numerical reflections of performance but signals that can shape a student's self-perception and learning trajectory.

Community-building grading practices include:

- **Formative feedback:** Prioritizing opportunities for students to revise and improve their work, thereby focusing on learning rather than punishment.
- **Transparent rubrics:** Offering clear criteria and expectations so that students understand how their work will be assessed.
- **Low-stakes assessments:** Incorporating quizzes, reflections, or practice assignments that help students build confidence without high pressure.
- **Narrative comments:** Providing contextualized explanations that go beyond symbols and grades, helping students see where they are improving and where they can grow.

By emphasizing mastery, self-reflection, and incremental progress, grading becomes a tool for leadership development. Students are not evaluated as fixed entities but as capable, evolving learners.

Inclusive Feedback Practices

Inclusivity in feedback means ensuring that every student, regardless of background, learning style, or ability, feels recognized, respected, and supported. Servant-leader faculty achieve this through:

- **Personalized tone:** Addressing students by name, acknowledging their specific effort, and avoiding generic or overly formulaic responses.
- **Cultural sensitivity:** Being mindful of how language may impact students from different backgrounds, and avoiding assumptions about prior knowledge or experiences.
- **Asset-based feedback:** Focusing on what students bring to the table, rather than what they lack, and guiding them to build on their strengths.
- **Emotionally intelligent responses:** Recognizing when students are struggling and responding with empathy rather than frustration or criticism.

Inclusivity also involves being receptive to feedback about grading practices. Servant-leader faculty may invite midterm reflections on what types of feedback students find most helpful, or offer anonymous comment forms to uncover unseen barriers.

When grading and feedback are delivered with intention and care, they become catalysts for connection. They show students that their efforts matter, their challenges are understood, and their growth is a shared goal.

Case Examples: Course Announcements and LMS Design Screenshots

To translate servant leadership from theory into actionable practice, we turn to concrete examples that illustrate how empathy, clarity, responsiveness, and empowerment can be embedded into the everyday operations of an online course.

These case studies highlight how simple yet intentional choices—such as crafting a thoughtful announcement or designing an intuitive LMS interface—can create a more human-centered and student-empowering digital learning experience.

When faculty members apply servant leadership principles to their teaching tools and communication strategies, they help foster inclusive, resilient, and values-driven classrooms.

Case Example 1: Course Announcement – Building Empathy and Community

In a fully online sociology course, a faculty member observes a notable decline in student participation and engagement midway through the semester. Several students have expressed feeling overwhelmed in discussion posts or email exchanges. Recognizing these patterns as a potential signal of rising academic and personal stress, the instructor uses the course announcement tool not just to inform, but to lead with compassion.

Announcement Title:

"Mid-Semester Check-In: You're Doing Better Than You Think!"

Announcement Body:

Hello everyone,

As we reach the midpoint of the semester, I want to take a moment to acknowledge the effort each of you has put into this course.

I know that this time of year can feel overwhelming—assignments, exams, work, and life responsibilities can pile up. Please know that you're not alone.

I see the hard work you're putting into your discussion posts, your assignments, and your growth as thinkers and leaders. If you're feeling stuck or behind, I encourage you to reach out. My virtual door is always open, and I'm here to help.

Remember, leadership isn't about being perfect. It's about showing up, learning from mistakes, and supporting others along the way. This week, consider checking in with a classmate or replying to someone who hasn't received much engagement on the boards.

Let's continue to support each other and finish the semester strong.

With appreciation,

[Instructor Name]

Servant Leadership Principles in Action:

- **Empathy:** The announcement acknowledges the emotional and academic weight students may be carrying, affirming that their struggles are seen and understood. This creates psychological safety and models emotional intelligence.
- **Encouragement:** By focusing on growth and effort rather than perfection, the instructor affirms students' progress, reinforcing intrinsic motivation and helping them reframe challenges as part of the learning journey.
- **Community-Building:** Encouraging peer-to-peer support in the discussion boards fosters a culture of

collaboration rather than competition, which can be especially critical in isolating online environments.

- **Availability and Support:** The instructor reaffirms their presence and approachability, offering help without judgment. This open invitation builds trust and reinforces a shared sense of responsibility for success.

Why It Matters:

What may appear to be a simple check-in message actually functions as a micro-leadership moment.

The tone, content, and timing of the announcement convey that the course is not just a sequence of tasks to be completed, but a shared experience in which the instructor actively cares about the whole student. Servant leadership is made real through this type of proactive communication—small gestures that make a big impact.

Case Example 2: LMS Design – Structuring for Student Empowerment and Clarity

A faculty member teaching an undergraduate public health course recognizes that students in virtual environments often feel disoriented or overwhelmed when navigating course materials.

To mitigate this, the instructor redesigns the course's learning management system (LMS) homepage to embody servant leadership values. Every element is intentionally chosen to reduce stress, promote independence, and support holistic student well-being.

LMS Homepage Features:

- **Welcome Video Introduction:** A 3-minute video from the instructor sets the tone. They share their teaching philosophy, what students can expect, and why the course matters in both academic and real-world contexts.

- **Clearly Organized Weekly Modules:** Each week's module is labeled by date, includes a brief overview of learning objectives, and links to all relevant assignments and readings in one place. Color-coded labels highlight due dates and workload expectations.

- **"Start Here" Orientation Module:** This essential section provides a course overview, syllabus, a video walkthrough of the LMS, and a student FAQ with common questions about grading, extensions, and course tools.

- **Student Support Resources:** A dedicated module includes links to academic advising, mental health services, writing and tutoring centers, as well as a "Questions & Answers" discussion board where students can support each other or seek guidance.

- **Reflection Journal Folder:** Students are invited to submit short, biweekly entries reflecting on what they're learning, their leadership development, and how the content relates to their goals and values.

Servant Leadership Principles Embedded in the Design:

- **Clarity and Transparency:** Reducing cognitive load is a form of service. By organizing content logically and explaining expectations clearly, the instructor removes barriers to learning and supports student autonomy.

- **Empowerment Through Self-Direction:** With resources and FAQs readily available, students can solve many of their own questions without needing constant instructor intervention—fostering confidence and independence.

- **Whole-Person Support:** Including mental health links and community discussion boards signals that the instructor sees students not only as learners but as human beings with diverse needs and challenges.

- **Encouraging Reflection:** The journal assignments move learning beyond rote content and invite students to engage in personal growth, self-awareness, and values clarification—hallmarks of servant leadership.

Why It Matters:

Online courses are often criticized for being impersonal or transactional.

By intentionally designing an LMS that supports emotional, cognitive, and social needs, this instructor transforms the digital platform into a vehicle for connection, growth, and empowerment. The LMS becomes not just a course shell, but a **servant-leader's classroom**—thoughtfully structured to meet students where they are.

These two case examples—the well-timed announcement and the student-centered LMS redesign—underscore an essential truth: servant leadership in education is lived through details. It shows up in how we design our syllabi, organize our digital tools, and communicate with care.

Whether through a simple message of encouragement or an intentionally crafted course homepage, faculty members have countless opportunities to model the values they want students to embody.

In servant-led classrooms, instructors are not distant evaluators, but *partners in learning*.

They lead by listening, by responding to real needs, and by building environments that nurture not just academic achievement but human development. Servant leadership transforms not only how courses are taught—but how students live, learn, and lead beyond the classroom.

Chapter 4: Asynchronous Student Leadership Development Activities

Leadership development is not confined to in-person interactions or formal titles.

In online higher education, especially within asynchronous environments, there are rich opportunities to foster leadership in creative, student-centered ways. This chapter explores practical, scalable activities that cultivate leadership qualities such as initiative, reflection, empathy, accountability, and collaboration.

Rather than positioning leadership as a distant goal or rare skillset, the servant leadership model encourages us to see leadership as a behavior—one that every student can practice and grow into. By integrating structured opportunities for students to lead, reflect, and support one another within the flow of regular course work, faculty can turn the online classroom into a transformative incubator for leadership development.

This first section focuses on two powerful strategies for asynchronous leadership cultivation: structured discussion forums with rotating peer leaders and student-led reflection threads. Each activity emphasizes both individual responsibility and community engagement, offering students the chance to learn by doing and to develop key competencies through practice.

Structuring Discussion Forums with Rotating Peer Leaders

Discussion forums are often seen as a static requirement in asynchronous courses—a space where students respond to prompts and check a box for participation. But when intentionally structured, these forums can become dynamic ecosystems where students not only engage with content but also take on leadership roles that develop critical thinking, collaboration, and communication skills.

One of the most effective methods to achieve this is by implementing a rotating peer leadership model.

What Are Rotating Peer Leaders?

Rotating peer leadership involves assigning students to facilitate weekly or biweekly discussion boards on a scheduled basis. Rather than having the instructor drive every conversation, students take turns guiding the dialogue, posing questions, summarizing discussions, and encouraging peer engagement.

This rotation transforms students from passive participants into active leaders. It gives them ownership of the learning process and builds confidence in their ability to lead academic discourse.

Implementing the Model

To implement rotating peer leaders effectively, faculty can follow these steps:

1. **Introduce the concept early:** Include a description of the peer leadership model in the syllabus and introduce it during the first week of class.
2. **Create a rotation schedule:** Assign each student a week (or topic) to lead. Consider group pairings if the class is large.
3. **Provide guidelines and expectations:** Outline what peer leaders are responsible for, such as:
    - Posting an original discussion prompt or elaborating on the weekly theme.
    - Responding to at least three classmates' posts with questions or insights.

- Posting a summary or wrap-up message highlighting key takeaways from the week.

4. **Offer support and models:** Share examples of effective discussion facilitation. Hold optional Zoom sessions or create videos to walk through expectations.

5. **Recognize contributions:** Publicly acknowledge the efforts of each peer leader. Offer private feedback that reinforces growth and identifies areas for improvement.

Benefits of Peer Leadership in Forums

This model aligns with several servant leadership principles:

- **Empowerment:** Students step into leadership roles in a safe, structured environment.

- **Listening and empathy:** Peer leaders practice attentiveness and engagement with others' perspectives.

- **Community-building:** The forums feel less like a monologue and more like a collaborative, co-owned space.

- **Reflection and foresight:** Leaders must anticipate how their questions might provoke insight, connection, or dialogue.

Moreover, rotating leadership distributes responsibility across the class. It prevents forums from becoming instructor-centered and encourages students to take intellectual risks.

Assessing Peer Leadership

To reinforce the value of this activity, peer leadership can be assessed using a simple rubric that includes:

- Clarity and thoughtfulness of the initial prompt.
- Depth and respectfulness of responses.
- Efforts to synthesize and guide conversation.
- Responsiveness to peer ideas.

Faculty can also include self-assessment and peer feedback forms, prompting students to reflect on their experience as a discussion leader and their engagement with peers.

This dual feedback mechanism supports growth and encourages a reflective approach to leadership.

Student-Led Reflection Threads

Reflection is a powerful tool in any educational context, but it takes on added significance in leadership development. Servant leadership requires self-awareness, humility, and a willingness to grow—all of which can be nurtured through structured reflection. In asynchronous learning, student-led reflection threads provide an accessible, community-oriented way to encourage leadership-minded introspection.

What Are Student-Led Reflection Threads?

Student-led reflection threads are an integral component of online learning that empower students to take charge of their own growth and leadership development.

These forums are dedicated spaces within the course where students post personal reflections about their leadership journey, growth experiences, or key insights from the course. Unlike content-based discussions driven by instructor prompts, student-led reflection threads allow learners to shape the conversation, driving both their personal development and peer engagement.

These threads typically operate as recurring spaces within the course, either weekly, biweekly, or tied to significant milestones in the learning process, such as after completing challenging assignments, presentations, or group projects. The idea behind these threads is to create opportunities for students to practice introspection and dialogue, develop leadership skills, and foster a deeper connection with the course content and their peers.

Structure and Implementation

To implement effective student-led reflection threads, faculty members must create a framework that guides the structure of these forums while allowing students the freedom to lead the conversation. The process typically includes the following elements:

1. Leadership Reflection Forum Introduction

The course should have a dedicated section or space titled something like "Leadership Reflection Forum" or "Personal Growth Reflection Thread," where students are invited to reflect on their leadership journey and growth. Faculty can introduce this as a recurring activity, explaining its purpose as an opportunity for students to engage in metacognitive thinking about their leadership skills, personal development, and the impact of course content.

This forum might be set up to encourage specific types of reflections at different points in the course:

- Reflecting on challenging moments that required leadership skills.
- Exploring instances where students felt empowered by the content or their actions.
- Analyzing shifts in their understanding of leadership and personal growth over time.

Each week, a student can volunteer or be assigned the responsibility of **starting the thread**. The student in this role has several tasks:

- **Post their own reflection:** The first post serves as the anchor for the discussion.

- **Ask an open-ended question:** To invite peers into the conversation and encourage others to share their reflections.

- **Engage with peers:** Respond to at least two other students' posts to foster community and peer mentorship.

2. Instructor's Role in Facilitating Reflection

Faculty involvement in the reflection threads should be supportive but not dominant. The key to these forums is maintaining a **student-led dynamic** where students feel free to express themselves and build upon each other's ideas.

Faculty comments should:

- **Affirm the student's growth:** Providing positive reinforcement for self-reflection and leadership insights.

- **Extend or guide** the conversation: Offering thoughtful questions or insights that encourage deeper reflection without overshadowing the student's voice.
- **Model active listening:** By responding thoughtfully to students' reflections, instructors demonstrate how to engage with others in a respectful and empathetic manner.

The goal is for instructors to **nurture** the conversation rather than take over it, creating a balanced and respectful exchange of ideas between students and the instructor.

Examples of Prompts for Reflection

While the structure of the reflection thread is open-ended, faculty can offer optional prompts to help students get started. These prompts can guide students toward thoughtful engagement with leadership concepts, personal growth, and course material.

Some examples of reflection prompts include:

- **"Describe a recent situation where you had to make a difficult decision. What guided your choice?"**

This prompt encourages students to reflect on their decision-making process, especially in leadership contexts, and how their values influenced those decisions.

- "How has your understanding of leadership evolved during this course?"

Students can consider how their views on leadership have developed over the duration of the course, integrating theoretical knowledge with real-life applications.

- "What strengths have you discovered in yourself through this course experience?"

This question helps students identify and articulate their personal growth, providing them with the opportunity to acknowledge their strengths and contributions to the class.

- "Who is a leader you admire and why? How do their values align with your own?"

Reflection on admired leaders not only invites students to reflect on the qualities they value in others but also prompts them to evaluate how those qualities align with their own emerging leadership styles.

Multimodal Engagement

Encouraging students to incorporate **multimodal elements**—such as images, quotes, videos, or music—can enhance the depth and creativity of their reflections. For example, a student might post a video clip from a TED Talk that inspired them or an image that symbolizes their leadership journey. By allowing students to explore different modes of expression, these threads not only become richer but also create opportunities for diverse learners to engage in the reflection process in ways that feel authentic to them.

Impact of Student-Led Reflections

Student-led reflection threads offer numerous benefits that go beyond the academic experience. These threads become transformative spaces where students can build important leadership skills, develop a sense of community, and grow personally.

1. Cultivating Voice

Reflection threads provide students with a platform to **articulate their values, challenges, and progress** in their own words. In doing so, they practice expressing themselves confidently and thoughtfully—an essential skill for effective leadership. By sharing their insights, students gain ownership over their learning process and develop a sense of agency in their personal and professional growth.

2. Fostering Vulnerability and Trust

Sharing personal insights and challenges in a safe, supportive environment helps **build trust** and encourages vulnerability. As students open up about their struggles or victories, they create a space for their peers to do the same. This vulnerability fosters deeper connections between students, leading to a stronger sense of community and shared experience.

3. Encouraging Peer Mentorship

Reflection threads naturally encourage **peer mentorship**. As students share their thoughts, they often provide advice, encouragement, or feedback to their classmates. This interaction promotes a **culture of support and collaboration**, where students help one another grow. Peer responses often lead to advice or shared experiences, helping students feel that they are not alone in their leadership journey.

4. Developing Metacognition

Metacognition—thinking about one's thinking—is a critical leadership skill. Reflection threads encourage students to evaluate their own thoughts, behaviors, and decision-making processes. By regularly engaging in this kind of reflection, students improve their ability to recognize patterns in their thinking and behavior, which is essential for personal development and leadership growth.

These threads can mirror practices from **traditional leadership training programs**, such as journaling or debriefing sessions, which encourage deep introspection about leadership experiences and lessons learned.

Integrating Assessment and Growth

While reflection threads should remain a space for open expression, **gentle evaluation** can help highlight their importance and ensure that students remain engaged with the process. Faculty may consider assessing participation in a **pass/fail format** based on the depth of engagement rather than content accuracy. This encourages students to prioritize personal growth over perfect performance.

Additionally, instructors can offer **occasional feedback** on students' reflections, providing constructive insights into their leadership development. This feedback should be framed positively and focus on how students can further refine their thinking or expand on their ideas.

As a **summative assessment** at the end of the course, students might be asked to submit a final reflection portfolio or synthesis essay. This might include:

- **A thematic analysis** of their reflections over the course of the term.
- **An evaluation of their leadership growth** and how their understanding of leadership has evolved.
- **An exploration of challenges** they encountered and how they responded to them as leaders.

This final reflection not only serves academic purposes but also acts as a **personal development artifact,** which students can carry with them as they move forward in their academic or professional lives.

Student-led reflection threads are not just an academic exercise—they are an essential tool for cultivating leadership skills, self-awareness, and personal growth. By creating spaces where students can reflect on their own leadership journey, engage with their peers, and receive support from their instructor, these threads contribute to a richer, more transformative learning experience. They are more than just discussions; they are opportunities for students to grow as leaders who are reflective, empathetic, and empowered to take action.

The first part of this chapter demonstrates that asynchronous learning is not a barrier to leadership development—it is an opportunity.

By creatively using tools such as discussion forums and reflection threads, faculty can give students structured chances to lead, think deeply, and grow. These activities foster a shared learning environment in which leadership is practiced by all, not reserved for a few.

In servant leadership, everyone is called to serve and support the growth of others. These student-led practices embody that ethos, making the online classroom a microcosm of the collaborative, compassionate leadership our world so deeply needs.

Leadership Roles in Group Projects

In asynchronous online courses, group projects provide a valuable platform for students to develop key leadership skills while working collaboratively in virtual settings. While online group work can present logistical challenges, it also offers unique opportunities to practice leadership in a flexible and adaptable environment.

When faculty intentionally structure leadership roles within group projects, students can better practice core leadership competencies, including organization, communication, empathy, and conflict resolution.

These experiences help students build the confidence and competence needed to lead effectively in future academic or professional settings.

Effective leadership in group projects requires clarity, accountability, and mutual respect. In an online environment where team members may not meet face-to-face, assigning specific leadership roles helps to clarify expectations, prevent unequal workload distribution, and foster a culture of collaboration and mutual accountability.

More importantly, these roles allow students to develop and demonstrate various leadership capacities in real-world contexts. By taking on different leadership roles in group projects, students learn valuable lessons about leading teams, managing diverse perspectives, and facilitating group success.

Key Leadership Roles in Group Projects

When assigning leadership roles in group projects, it's essential to define roles clearly, making sure each student has an opportunity to contribute meaningfully. Below are three commonly effective leadership roles that align with the principles of servant leadership, which emphasizes collaboration, empathy, and support for others' growth.

1. Discussion Facilitator

The role of the Discussion Facilitator is critical in promoting productive dialogue and ensuring the group stays focused on the task at hand.

- **Responsibilities:**

- Initiates and maintains group discussions by posting thoughtful questions and engaging conversation starters.
- Ensures that everyone in the group has an opportunity to participate, encouraging quieter members to contribute.
- Keeps discussions on track, ensuring they stay relevant to the assignment goals.
- Promotes respectful, inclusive dialogue and mediates if discussions become unproductive or contentious.

This role emphasizes communication and collaboration—two fundamental elements of servant leadership.

By facilitating group discussions, students learn how to synthesize ideas, listen actively, and keep the group focused on collective goals. This role also requires patience and diplomacy, as the facilitator must navigate diverse opinions and manage group dynamics.

The Discussion Facilitator becomes responsible for ensuring that all voices are heard and that the group moves toward shared understanding and decision-making.

2. Conflict Navigator

In group work, especially in diverse online settings, disagreements and misunderstandings are bound to arise. The Conflict Navigator plays a crucial role in maintaining harmony within the group by mediating disputes and ensuring that tensions do not derail the project.

Responsibilities:

- Acts as the mediator when conflicts or communication breakdowns occur within the group.
- Keeps the tone of discussions constructive, encouraging positive communication and resolution.
- Helps resolve disagreements by identifying underlying concerns and facilitating compromise or consensus.
- In cases where conflicts cannot be resolved internally, works with the instructor to address the issue and ensure the group can continue working effectively.

The Conflict Navigator's role is to embody emotional intelligence and diplomacy. This student leader must approach conflicts with empathy, respect, and a focus on solutions rather than blame.

In addition, the Conflict Navigator helps ensure that the group's collaboration is inclusive and that all members feel valued. This role teaches students the importance of managing relationships and resolving tension in ways that promote group cohesion and productivity. It aligns with the principles of servant leadership by prioritizing the well-being of the group and fostering healthy, supportive relationships among team members.

3. Resource Curator

The Resource Curator is responsible for gathering, organizing, and sharing academic resources that support the group's project. This role ensures that the group's work is grounded in credible, high-quality research and that the project stays aligned with academic standards.

Responsibilities:

- Identifies and organizes academic resources such as articles, books, research studies, and other materials that are relevant to the project.
- Ensures that all sources used in the project are credible and properly documented to maintain the academic integrity of the work.
- Helps integrate research into the group's work, ensuring that it is both applicable and properly cited.
- Keeps the group informed about any updates or new resources that could strengthen the project.

The Resource Curator fosters stewardship and foresight—two key attributes of servant leadership. By ensuring that the group uses well-researched and credible sources, the Resource Curator demonstrates a commitment to quality and integrity.

This role also requires organizational skills and attention to detail to ensure that all resources are properly integrated into the final project. The role of the Resource Curator reinforces the idea that leadership is not only about directing others but also about supporting the collective effort through diligence and accountability.

Supporting Role-Based Learning

To ensure that leadership roles in group projects are meaningful and effective, faculty should provide support and guidance throughout the project. This support helps students understand the purpose of each role and how to execute it effectively. Here are a few strategies to support role-based learning in group projects:

1. Provide Role Descriptions

Each leadership role should be clearly defined, with specific responsibilities outlined. Faculty can provide a brief description of each role, explaining the expectations and key tasks associated with it. This helps students understand their responsibilities and ensures that the roles are executed effectively.

2. Offer Performance Checklists or Rubrics

To guide students in their leadership roles, faculty can provide performance checklists or rubrics that detail the criteria for success. This may include specific actions the student should take (e.g., initiating discussion, resolving conflicts, gathering resources) and how their performance will be evaluated. Providing clear criteria helps students understand how their efforts contribute to the group's success and how they will be assessed.

3. Encourage Goal-Setting

At the beginning of each project, encourage students to set personal leadership goals related to their roles. For example, the Discussion Facilitator might set a goal to post a check-in message every three days, or the Conflict Navigator might aim to mediate any conflicts promptly. Goal-setting helps students stay focused on their responsibilities and gives them something to strive for throughout the project.

4. Create Group Reflection Forums

Provide optional reflection forums for students to discuss their leadership experiences within their groups. These forums can be used for students to share insights, challenges, and successes related to their roles. Faculty can facilitate these discussions by prompting students to reflect on how their roles influenced group dynamics, collaboration, and project outcomes. Reflection forums promote self-awareness and growth, allowing students to learn from their experiences and refine their leadership skills.

Assessment Strategies for Leadership Roles

Evaluating leadership in group projects requires a holistic approach that considers both individual contributions and the overall effectiveness of the group's collaboration. Faculty should incorporate a range of assessment strategies to ensure that leadership is recognized and developed. These strategies may include:

1. Reflections on Leadership Roles

Students can reflect on their experiences in their leadership roles, answering questions such as:

- What did I learn from taking on this leadership role?
- What challenges did I encounter, and how did I address them?
- How did I serve my group and contribute to its success?

These reflections allow students to assess their own leadership growth and identify areas for improvement.

2. Peer Feedback

In addition to self-reflection, peer feedback provides valuable insight into how well each student performed in their leadership role. Peers can evaluate each other based on specific criteria, such as communication, collaboration, conflict resolution, and resource management. Peer evaluations can be conducted through anonymous surveys or group discussions.

3. Group Evaluations

At the conclusion of the project, a group evaluation can be conducted to assess overall leadership and collaboration. This evaluation can include criteria such as:

- How effectively did the group communicate and collaborate?
- How well did the leadership roles contribute to the group's success?
- How did each member contribute to the project's completion and success?

This evaluation helps students appreciate the importance of each leadership role and how collaboration is essential for group success.

Leadership roles in group projects provide a powerful opportunity for students to practice and develop key leadership competencies in an online learning environment.

By assigning specific roles such as Discussion Facilitator, Conflict Navigator, and Resource Curator, faculty create an intentional structure that fosters accountability, communication, and collaboration.

These roles align well with the principles of servant leadership, ensuring that students not only develop their own leadership abilities but also contribute to the growth and success of their peers.

Through structured role-based learning and thoughtful assessment strategies, students gain the skills, confidence, and self-awareness needed to lead effectively in diverse and collaborative settings.

Peer Mentoring Programs Within Courses

Peer mentoring is a powerful, underutilized approach to leadership development in asynchronous online learning. When structured effectively, peer mentoring provides students with a supportive relationship where they can grow academically, emotionally, and professionally.

Within a course, peer mentoring can take many forms. Whether formalized (as a standing program) or informal (arising from instructor-facilitated connections), mentoring relationships give students the opportunity to practice listening, guiding, supporting, and empowering others—hallmarks of servant leadership.

Models of Peer Mentoring

1. **Experienced Mentors for New Students**
    - In multi-cohort programs or recurring courses, experienced students from past cohorts may return as mentors.
    - These students can be offered extra credit, a digital badge, or a small stipend.
    - Mentors are introduced during the first week and may host Q&A forums, review assignments, or provide encouragement.

2. **Intra-course Peer Buddies**
    - Students are paired early in the course and encouraged to check in regularly via email, discussion posts, or messaging apps.
    - Responsibilities may include providing feedback on drafts, sharing strategies for time

management, or reflecting together on course takeaways.

3. **Mentoring Pods**
    - Small groups of 3-5 students work together throughout the course.
    - Each week, one member serves as the "mentor-of-the-week," checking in on others, curating helpful tips, or starting a motivational thread.

Each of these models builds community while offering repeated, structured opportunities for students to lead, support, and grow.

Structuring Mentoring Activities

For mentoring to be meaningful, it needs a clear structure and purpose. Consider including:

- A "Peer Mentoring Guide" with conversation starters, do's and don'ts, and reflective activities.
- Discussion forums designated for mentors and mentees.
- Occasional check-ins or short reflection surveys to assess the mentoring experience.

- Encouragement for mentors to model vulnerability and share their own learning journeys.

Mentors should not be expected to replace faculty support or provide academic instruction. Their role is relational and developmental—helping peers feel seen, heard, and capable.

The Leadership Impact of Mentoring

Peer mentors often experience the most growth. By supporting others, they develop their capacity for:

- **Empathy and emotional intelligence:** Learning to understand and respond to the diverse needs of peers.
- **Communication:** Practicing how to offer guidance in respectful and constructive ways.
- **Listening and feedback:** Developing the ability to give and receive insight effectively.
- **Confidence:** Stepping into a leadership identity and seeing the positive impact of their actions.

For mentees, mentoring reduces isolation, increases resilience, and fosters a sense of belonging. These outcomes contribute directly to academic success and personal growth.

Faculty Role and Support

Faculty do not need to manage every interaction but should:

- Introduce and endorse the program.
- Be available to mentor mentors when questions arise.
- Offer reflective prompts that encourage students to process the mentoring experience.
- Celebrate milestones and recognize exemplary mentors in course communications.

These student leadership strategies—whether through clearly defined roles in group projects or thoughtfully structured peer mentoring—advance the servant leadership goal of shared growth, empowerment, and ethical development. By making leadership visible, actionable, and integral to online course design, faculty help students see themselves not only as learners but as capable contributors to their learning communities.

As we continue this chapter, we will explore additional ways to engage students in leadership development, ensuring that the asynchronous environment is not a barrier, but a launchpad for personal and interpersonal growth.

Online leadership reflection journals or blogs.

Reflection is a critical component of servant leadership, and in asynchronous learning, digital journals or blogs serve as powerful tools for leadership development. By engaging students in structured self-reflection, faculty help learners internalize course concepts, assess their personal growth, and articulate their leadership values and goals.

Structure and Purpose

Online reflection journals can be integrated into the LMS or hosted on external platforms like Google Docs, WordPress, or class discussion threads. Students post entries weekly, biweekly, or following major course milestones. These reflections can include prompts such as:

- Describe a time you practiced leadership in this course.
- What challenges have tested your leadership values?
- How are you developing empathy, listening, or foresight?
- What leadership strengths have you discovered in yourself?

Reflection blogs may be public (shared with the class) or private (shared only with the instructor), depending on course culture and student comfort. Instructors may provide guiding questions or allow open-ended formats, enabling students to reflect on what matters most to them.

Benefits of Leadership Journals

- **Metacognition:** Students gain awareness of their behaviors, choices, and growth areas.
- **Accountability:** Regular entries build a practice of discipline and self-directed learning.
- **Authentic assessment:** Instructors can evaluate both leadership progression and writing skills.
- **Empathy and perspective-taking:** Reading peers' reflections (in public blogs) enhances understanding and community.

Faculty feedback should validate effort and insight while gently challenging students to go deeper. Periodic summary reflections or a final leadership growth essay can help students synthesize their journey.

Mock Crisis-Response Simulations

Leadership is often most clearly demonstrated in times of crisis, where decisions must be made swiftly, ethically, and collaboratively. Online mock crisis-response simulations offer a unique and immersive learning experience that challenges students to apply leadership competencies in high-pressure, complex, and uncertain environments. These simulations not only test decision-making skills but also encourage teamwork, ethical reasoning, and clear communication—all essential qualities of effective leadership.

Mock crisis-response simulations can be integrated into online courses to help students practice handling real-world scenarios and gain valuable experience in leading under stress. These simulations provide an experiential learning environment where students can engage in decision-making, adapt to new information, and reflect on their leadership decisions in a controlled, academic setting.

Designing Crisis Simulations

Effective crisis simulations require careful planning to ensure that the scenario is engaging, realistic, and provides opportunities for leadership development. Key components of a crisis-response simulation include:

1. A Detailed Scenario

The scenario should be complex, relevant, and immersive, providing students with a realistic crisis that requires quick thinking and decisive leadership. Examples of scenarios include:

- **A Campus Cyberattack:** A simulated cyberattack on a university's IT systems disrupts academic and administrative functions, and students must respond with strategic communication, data protection, and crisis management.

- **A Public Health Emergency:** A sudden outbreak of a contagious disease requires immediate responses involving public safety measures, communication with health organizations, and leadership in managing a community response.

- **An Organizational Scandal:** A high-profile company or organization is embroiled in an ethical scandal, and students must navigate public relations, internal team communication, and damage control.

The scenario should be detailed enough to provide a clear context but leave enough ambiguity for students to make decisions, demonstrate leadership, and manage unforeseen complications.

2. Defined Roles

In a mock crisis simulation, students should take on distinct leadership roles to ensure a diversity of perspectives and skills. These roles might include:

- **Communications Director:** Responsible for managing internal and external messaging, creating press releases, and responding to media inquiries.

- **Student Leader:** Takes on the role of a representative of the broader student body, leading communications and response strategies on behalf of students.

- **Ethics Officer:** Ensures that all decisions are ethically sound, and that the organization or group responds in a manner consistent with its values.

- **Operations Manager:** Oversees the logistical aspects of the crisis response, coordinating team efforts and managing resources.

- **Legal Advisor:** Provides guidance on the legal implications of decisions made during the crisis and ensures that responses adhere to relevant regulations.

These roles encourage collaboration and negotiation, as students must work together while also assuming responsibility for different facets of the response. Rotating roles or allowing students to choose their roles based on their interests can also enhance engagement.

3. Timed Phases

To replicate the fast-paced nature of real-world crises, simulations should unfold over multiple stages, with each phase requiring analysis, response, and adaptation. The instructor can introduce time constraints to mimic the urgency that often accompanies real-world crises. For example:

- **Phase 1: Crisis Identification:** Students are given the scenario and initial details about the crisis. They must assess the situation, decide on an initial response, and communicate with relevant stakeholders.

- **Phase 2: Response Strategy:** After gathering more information or receiving updates, students must refine their strategies and decide on specific actions (e.g., press conferences, internal briefings, policy changes).

- **Phase 3: Aftermath and Reflection:** The crisis reaches a resolution, and students reflect on the outcomes of their decisions, how well they managed the crisis, and what they would do differently in the future.

Throughout the simulation, instructors can add complications or plot twists—such as new information or stakeholder reactions—to increase the challenge and require students to adapt their strategies on the fly.

4. Deliverables

In crisis simulations, students must produce tangible outcomes that reflect their leadership and decision-making processes. These deliverables might include:

- **Press Releases:** Students act as the communications director and draft official statements to address the public and media.

- **Internal Memos:** Students in leadership roles within the organization may create memos to brief colleagues on the ongoing crisis and decisions taken.

- **Video Statements:** Students may record video responses or public addresses, simulating live leadership communication.

- **Policy Recommendations:** As a part of the simulation, students may be tasked with providing actionable policy recommendations to address the root cause of the crisis or mitigate future risks.

The deliverables serve as tangible markers of student performance, showcasing their ability to respond effectively and lead under pressure.

Leadership Competencies Developed

Mock crisis simulations are effective tools for developing a wide range of leadership competencies. These include:

1. Foresight and Decision-Making

Crisis simulations require students to make decisions with limited information, anticipating potential consequences and considering a variety of options. Effective leaders must be able to think ahead, weighing the long-term impacts of their decisions while balancing immediate needs. The simulation forces students to apply critical thinking skills and to prioritize actions that align with the organization's values and objectives.

2. Ethical Reasoning

Crisis scenarios often present ethical dilemmas with no easy solutions. Students must balance competing priorities, such as transparency versus privacy, or urgency versus thoroughness. These challenges provide valuable opportunities for students to apply ethical reasoning in complex situations, considering the impact of their decisions on different stakeholders and upholding their integrity as leaders.

3. Communication Skills

Clear, concise, and effective communication is a cornerstone of leadership, especially during a crisis. Students must practice communicating with different audiences under pressure, adjusting their tone, style, and message depending on the context (e.g., internal teams, the public, or external partners). This skill is critical in maintaining trust, mitigating panic, and ensuring that responses are understood and acted upon effectively.

4. Team Dynamics

Effective leadership is often about **collaboration** and **negotiating team roles**. In crisis simulations, students must collaborate with peers to create a coordinated response. They learn how to manage diverse perspectives, resolve conflicts, and negotiate roles to ensure that everyone's strengths are utilized effectively. This is especially important in high-stakes situations where group cohesion and collaboration can make or break the response effort.

Debriefing and Reflection

Post-simulation reflection is essential for students to analyze their leadership decisions and evaluate the effectiveness of their strategies. The debriefing process allows students to learn from their experiences, identify areas for improvement, and connect their actions to servant leadership principles.

Sample reflection prompts include:

- What leadership traits did you rely on most during the simulation?

- How did your group handle disagreement or ambiguity? What strategies did you use to resolve conflicts or align team members?

- What would you do differently if you were to respond to a real-world crisis scenario?

- How did your decision-making process align with the principles of servant leadership, such as empathy, collaboration, and ethical reasoning?

These questions encourage students to reflect on both their successes and challenges, fostering growth and continuous improvement.

Assessment of Simulations

The assessment of mock crisis simulations should reflect both the process and the outcome of the students' leadership efforts. Evaluation may include:

- **Participation**: Engaging actively in the simulation, including posting reflections, contributing to group discussions, and completing deliverables.

- **Deliverables**: The quality, clarity, and appropriateness of materials produced (e.g., press releases, memos, policy recommendations).

- **Peer Evaluations:** Peer feedback on individual contributions and teamwork during the simulation.

- **Reflective Writing:** A final reflection or synthesis essay where students analyze their leadership growth, evaluate the effectiveness of their strategies, and discuss lessons learned.

Mock crisis-response simulations offer a powerful experiential learning opportunity for students to develop essential leadership competencies, such as decision-making, communication, ethical reasoning, and teamwork.

By immersing students in realistic, high-pressure scenarios, these simulations provide a platform for leadership development that is applicable both in academic contexts and in real-world professional settings.

With effective debriefing and reflection, students gain deeper insights into their leadership strengths and areas for improvement, preparing them for future leadership roles in a complex and dynamic world.

Example Activity Templates and Assessment Rubrics

For leadership activities to be effective and scalable, faculty need concrete tools to support their implementation. Below are templates and rubrics to guide discussion forums, peer leadership, mentoring, and reflection.

Template: Peer Leadership Discussion Forum

Week X Peer Leader Guidelines:

- Post a discussion question or thematic quote by Monday.
- Reply to at least 3 classmates with thoughtful follow-ups.
- Summarize key takeaways in a wrap-up post by Sunday.

Tips:

- Encourage diverse perspectives.
- Ask open-ended questions.
- Highlight peers' contributions.

Rubric: Peer Leadership Performance (10 points)

Criteria	Excellent (3)	Satisfactory (2)	Needs Improvement (1)

Prompt Quality	Clear, engaging, relevant	Adequate, basic relevance	Vague, confusing
Engagement	3+ insightful responses	2 basic responses	1 or fewer responses
Synthesis	Wrap-up shows depth and inclusion	Basic summary provided	Little or no synthesis
Tone and Respect	Positive, inclusive, thoughtful	Generally respectful	Disengaged or dismissive

Template: Reflection Journal Prompts

- Describe a leadership challenge you faced this week.
- How are you applying course principles in your life or work?
- What feedback have you received, and how are you responding to it?

Assessment Criteria:

- Frequency (weekly or biweekly).
- Depth of thought.
- Connection to course themes.
- Growth over time.

Template: Peer Mentoring Guide

Initial Tasks:

- Introduce yourself to your mentee.
- Set communication preferences (email, LMS message, Zoom).
- Share 3 tips for success in this course.

Ongoing Ideas:

- Discuss time management and study strategies.
- Encourage reflection on assignments.
- Celebrate milestones together.

Mentor Reflection Prompts:

- What have you learned from supporting a peer?
- What surprised you about your mentee?
- How are you growing as a servant leader?

By integrating these activities, templates, and assessment tools, faculty empower students to engage deeply with leadership practice. Servant leadership is about creating conditions where others can flourish—and every aspect of an asynchronous classroom, when designed with intention, can support that mission.

Chapter 5: Faculty Self-Assessment and Reflection

As online educators strive to create meaningful learning experiences rooted in servant leadership, a foundational yet often overlooked component is self-awareness.

Servant leadership, by its very nature, demands that leaders consistently reflect on their motives, practices, and growth.

In the context of online higher education, faculty must examine how their behaviors, course design decisions, and communication styles reflect—or misalign with—the servant leadership values they aim to model.

This chapter explores why faculty self-awareness is central to effective leadership modeling and offers practical tools for self-assessment and reflection.

The goal is not to prescribe perfection, but to foster an ongoing process of learning, humility, and purposeful growth. When faculty engage in regular self-reflection, they model vulnerability and adaptability, creating an environment where students also feel empowered to grow.

Why Faculty Self-Awareness Matters in Leadership Modeling

In the realm of online education, leadership extends far beyond the content delivered or the structure of the course. It encompasses how faculty engage with students, the manner in which they communicate, and the energy and intentions they bring to their teaching.

Self-awareness in faculty members plays a pivotal role in shaping these elements. It is not merely about what faculty do, but about how and why they do it.

In online classrooms, where tone, clarity, and presence can deeply influence the student experience, unexamined habits or assumptions can inadvertently undermine trust, empathy, or engagement.

Faculty who are self-aware recognize their influence, assess their impact, and make intentional choices to align their teaching with their core values. This self-reflection and ongoing development enhance not only the learning experience but also the faculty's own growth, leading to more effective teaching and positive student outcomes.

The Importance of Self-Awareness for Faculty Leadership

Self-awareness involves an ongoing process of introspection, reflection, and growth.

For faculty members, this means continuously evaluating their teaching practices, communication styles, and emotional responses to students. In an online environment, where interactions are often limited to written communication and asynchronous formats, the nuances of faculty leadership become even more crucial.

The impact of leadership is felt not just through direct instruction but through the ways faculty model behaviors, decisions, and attitudes. When faculty are self-aware, they are better equipped to navigate the complexities of teaching, foster a positive learning environment, and maintain their own well-being in the process.

How Faculty Self-Awareness Enhances Authenticity

One of the most profound benefits of self-awareness for faculty is the enhancement of their authenticity. Authenticity is vital in building trust and rapport with students, and it is particularly important in an online setting, where face-to-face interactions are limited.

Self-aware instructors are more likely to teach from a place of personal understanding and confidence. When faculty are clear about their values, teaching philosophies, strengths, and areas for growth, they can engage with students in a more open and genuine way.

Authentic teaching creates an environment where students feel seen and heard. This transparency in communication helps students connect with instructors as real, relatable individuals rather than distant or impersonal figures.

In the absence of physical presence, such relational trust becomes a cornerstone of the student experience. When faculty model authenticity, they inspire students to adopt similar openness in their own learning processes, leading to a deeper level of engagement and collaboration.

Improving Emotional Intelligence in Online Learning

Emotional intelligence (EQ) is a critical skill for faculty members, especially in an online classroom where nonverbal cues are often absent. Self-aware faculty members are better equipped to interpret students' emotional needs, even through text-based communication.

Understanding their own emotional responses allows instructors to recognize when they are feeling frustrated, overwhelmed, or disengaged—emotions that could inadvertently influence their interactions with students. By being attuned to their own feelings, self-aware faculty can respond to students with greater empathy and emotional intelligence.

In online learning environments, where students may feel isolated or disconnected, faculty members who exhibit emotional intelligence can be the difference between a student feeling supported or abandoned.

Whether it's responding to an emotionally charged email, offering encouragement after a tough assignment, or recognizing when a student is struggling without explicitly stating it, emotionally intelligent faculty are able to guide their students with sensitivity and care. This kind of responsiveness is foundational to building a learning environment where students feel safe and motivated to engage in deep, meaningful learning.

Supporting Reflective Practice and Continuous Growth

Self-awareness fosters a habit of reflective practice, which is essential for improving teaching effectiveness. Faculty members who are committed to self-awareness regularly assess the impact of their teaching strategies, the effectiveness of their communication, and the alignment of their course design with student needs.

Rather than simply going through the motions of instruction, these instructors consistently evaluate their practices to ensure that they are serving their students' best interests.

Self-aware educators are open to feedback, whether from students, peers, or their own introspection. They are willing to experiment with new approaches and reflect on their successes and failures.

For example, if a certain teaching method is not resonating with students or if engagement in discussion forums is low, self-aware faculty members will take the time to revise and adapt their approach. This commitment to reflective practice not only improves the learning experience but also encourages a culture of ongoing improvement.

Moreover, faculty who model reflective practice also encourage students to do the same. By demonstrating that learning is a continual process of growth, faculty foster a mindset in which students are encouraged to assess their own progress, identify areas for improvement, and actively engage in their own development.

Modeling Growth Mindset for Students

Self-awareness in faculty also plays a critical role in modeling a growth mindset for students. A growth mindset, as popularized by psychologist Carol Dweck, is the belief that abilities and intelligence can be developed through dedication and hard work. Faculty members who are self-aware engage in their own learning journey, showing that growth is not only possible but essential. When faculty share their own challenges, failures, and learning processes, they reinforce the idea that mistakes are opportunities for growth, not reflections of fixed abilities.

This modeling of a growth mindset has a powerful impact on students. When students see faculty members struggling with new ideas or making adjustments to their teaching methods, it helps them understand that learning is a dynamic, iterative process.

It encourages students to approach challenges with resilience and persistence rather than fear of failure. In essence, faculty who model a growth mindset demonstrate that leadership is about continuous improvement, self-reflection, and a commitment to learning.

Preventing Burnout and Misalignment

Another critical benefit of self-awareness for faculty is its role in preventing burnout and ensuring alignment with personal values. The demands of teaching—especially in an online environment—can be overwhelming, with faculty juggling multiple courses, administrative tasks, and student needs.

Self-aware faculty members are better able to recognize when they are nearing burnout or when they feel misaligned with their values. They can assess whether the demands of their teaching role are taking a toll on their well-being or causing them to disengage from their core mission as educators.

Through regular self-reflection, faculty can identify early signs of burnout and take proactive steps to recalibrate their work-life balance, adjust their teaching practices, or set boundaries with students.

Self-awareness helps faculty recognize when they are stretching themselves too thin and need to take time for self-care or professional development. This ability to self-regulate is essential for maintaining long-term effectiveness as an educator.

Additionally, faculty who regularly reflect on their values and teaching practices are better equipped to stay true to their core mission as educators.

They are less likely to become bogged down by administrative tasks, institutional pressures, or external expectations that conflict with their teaching philosophy. This alignment between personal values and professional practice contributes to greater job satisfaction and a more meaningful connection to students.

Self-awareness is a foundational element of effective leadership in online education. It enhances authenticity, improves emotional intelligence, fosters reflective practice, and models a growth mindset for students.

By being attuned to their own emotional responses, strengths, and areas for growth, faculty members can lead in a way that is genuine, empathetic, and impactful. Furthermore, self-aware faculty are better equipped to prevent burnout and ensure their teaching remains aligned with their values.

Ultimately, self-awareness allows faculty members to be more intentional in their approach to teaching and leadership. It empowers them to create a learning environment that fosters trust, encourages growth, and promotes meaningful student engagement.

As faculty continue to model the importance of self-awareness, they cultivate an atmosphere where both students and educators can grow together, fostering a culture of lifelong learning, reflection, and personal development.

Servant Leadership Self-Assessment Tools

While self-awareness can emerge through informal reflection, structured tools can deepen insights and provide a foundation for intentional growth. Below are several types of self-assessment instruments that faculty can use to examine their leadership behaviors in the online classroom.

1. Servant Leadership Self-Inventory (SLSI)

This tool asks faculty to rate themselves on key servant leadership dimensions, such as:

- Listening
- Empathy
- Healing
- Awareness
- Persuasion
- Conceptualization
- Foresight
- Stewardship
- Commitment to the growth of others
- Building community

Sample items:

- "I actively seek to understand the needs of my students before responding."
- "I design my course to support the long-term growth of each student, not just content mastery."

- "I create opportunities for students to lead and collaborate."

Faculty can score their responses on a Likert scale (e.g., 1 = Rarely, 5 = Consistently) and reflect on strengths and areas for development.

2. Weekly Reflection Template

This brief, recurring tool prompts faculty to evaluate how they modeled servant leadership during the past week. Sample prompts include:

- "How did I show empathy toward students this week?"
- "Where did I miss an opportunity to listen more fully or respond more compassionately?"
- "What leadership values did I emphasize in my announcements or feedback?"

Reflection entries can be compiled into a semester-long growth journal, allowing patterns and progress to emerge.

3. Student Feedback Surveys

In addition to institutional evaluations, faculty can design informal surveys that ask students to reflect on leadership dynamics in the course.

Sample questions:

- "Do you feel heard and respected in this course? Why or why not?"
- "How well does the instructor support your growth beyond just academic performance?"
- "What actions by the instructor make you feel part of a community?"

These surveys can be anonymous and administered mid-semester to provide real-time insights for adjustment.

4. Peer Observation and Dialogue

Inviting a colleague to observe an online course and provide feedback through the lens of servant leadership can offer invaluable perspective. Faculty pairs can:

- Exchange syllabi or announcements.
- Observe a module and review LMS structure.
- Offer feedback on how values like empathy, clarity, and community are (or are not) expressed.

This peer dialogue approach fosters accountability, reflection, and mutual support.

5. Values Clarification Exercise

Faculty can periodically revisit their personal and professional values using tools such as:

- A "values card sort" to prioritize guiding principles.
- A reflection prompt: "What three values are at the core of my teaching practice?"
- A visualization: "What kind of leader do I want my students to become, and how do I model that daily?"

This grounding process helps align everyday decisions with long-term goals.

Faculty self-assessment is not a one-time event. It is an ongoing discipline that nurtures humility, integrity, and growth. By engaging with tools like the ones described here, online educators not only refine their practice but also deepen their impact.

In the next section of this chapter, we will explore how faculty can use their self-assessment insights to create personal development plans that sustain and expand their servant leadership journey.

Reflection prompts for online faculty.

While self-assessment tools provide a structured approach to introspection, reflection prompts offer a more fluid and creative pathway to faculty insight. These prompts serve as intellectual and emotional doorways into self-discovery, professional growth, and leadership development. For online faculty committed to practicing servant leadership, regular reflection can reveal subtle shifts in mindset, tone, empathy, and engagement.

Prompts can be used in weekly teaching journals, end-of-module reviews, or even in casual note-taking after key teaching moments. Below is a categorized set of prompts designed specifically for online educators integrating servant leadership principles.

Prompts on Empathy and Student Support

- When did I last reach out to a struggling student? How did I show care?
- How am I supporting students who are managing invisible challenges (work, caregiving, mental health)?
- Have I assumed anything about my students' experiences that I need to revisit?

Prompts on Listening and Responsiveness

- How do I ensure I truly "listen" to student questions, even in asynchronous formats?
- What methods do I use to invite feedback from my students? How do I act on that feedback?
- What recent interaction demonstrated my commitment to listening over reacting?

Prompts on Communication Style

- What tone do I adopt in my announcements, emails, and feedback? What does that tone communicate about my leadership?
- Have I made space for humor, vulnerability, or warmth in my communication?
- Am I consistent in responding to students with respect and encouragement?

Prompts on Course Design and Flexibility

- In what ways does my course design honor student autonomy and different learning styles?
- How do I incorporate flexibility without sacrificing academic rigor?
- How am I using the LMS to support clarity, inclusion, and accessibility?

Prompts on Modeling Leadership Values

- What leadership qualities do I hope my students develop, and how do I embody them?
- How have I modeled resilience or ethical decision-making this term?

- Have I been transparent about my own learning journey as an educator?

Prompts on Growth and Improvement

- What patterns am I noticing in my reflections this semester?
- What recurring challenges suggest areas for my development?
- What successes am I most proud of, and what made them possible?

By consistently engaging with such questions, faculty create a narrative of leadership development that is both personalized and purpose-driven. They begin to understand not only what they do but why and how they do it—the essence of reflective servant leadership.

Creating a Personal Servant Leadership Development Plan

Leadership development is a continuous, evolving process. Faculty who seek to embody servant leadership—an approach that prioritizes the growth and well-being of others—need a structured, intentional approach to growing in this role.

While reflection and self-assessment are critical first steps, translating these insights into a personal leadership development plan is key for sustained growth.

A personal servant leadership development plan is not a static checklist of goals but rather a dynamic, evolving document that outlines intentional strategies for leadership growth and impact. By regularly revisiting and revising this plan, faculty can ensure that their leadership journey remains aligned with their values, goals, and evolving pedagogical approaches.

Why Create a Personal Servant Leadership Development Plan?

A personal servant leadership development plan serves multiple functions:

- **Translate Reflection into Action:** Reflection alone does not lead to growth unless it is paired with intentional actions. This plan transforms insights from self-assessment and reflection into concrete, measurable steps toward improvement.

- **Track Patterns and Shifts Over Time:** By having a written plan, faculty can track their leadership development, noticing patterns, progress, and areas that may need further attention. Over time, this allows them to recognize growth or identify recurring challenges.

- **Set Realistic, Meaningful Goals Aligned with Values:** A servant leadership development plan helps faculty set goals that are deeply rooted in their core values. These goals should be specific, measurable, and achievable while also aligned with broader leadership principles.

- **Commit to Continual Learning:** A personal leadership plan promotes a mindset of ongoing learning. Faculty will be encouraged to continually assess their leadership practices, adapt their strategies, and embrace growth in both leadership and pedagogy.

Components of a Personal Servant Leadership Development Plan

The plan should be tailored to the individual faculty member's leadership philosophy, course design, and teaching practices. Here are key components that help build a comprehensive, actionable plan:

1. Personal Mission Statement

A Personal Mission Statement serves as the foundation of the development plan. It encapsulates the faculty member's overarching "why" as both an educator and a leader. It acts as a guide to align decisions, actions, and goals with personal values and principles.

Example Mission Statement:

"To create inclusive, empowering online learning environments where every student feels seen, challenged, and inspired, fostering their growth as thoughtful, engaged, and ethical leaders."

This mission statement provides clarity on the faculty member's purpose and priorities, and serves as a touchstone for evaluating decisions and actions throughout their leadership journey.

2. Leadership Values Inventory

A **Leadership Values Inventory** helps faculty identify the core values that shape their leadership approach. These values inform teaching practices, interactions with students, and leadership decisions. By understanding these guiding principles, faculty can remain grounded in their leadership approach, even when faced with challenges.

- **Suggested Values for Inventory:**
  - **Empathy:** Understanding and sharing the feelings of others to foster trust and understanding in communication.

- **Equity:** Ensuring fair treatment and opportunities for all students, regardless of background or ability.
- **Humility:** Acknowledging the inherent worth and potential of all individuals and remaining open to learning from others.
- **Resilience:** The ability to persist in the face of challenges and setbacks while modeling perseverance for students.
- **Collaboration:** Recognizing that leadership is not about individual achievement but fostering collective growth through cooperation.

Reflecting on these values regularly helps faculty ensure their teaching aligns with their personal leadership philosophy and their students' needs.

3. Strengths and Growth Areas

Recognizing both **strengths** and **growth areas** is essential to developing an authentic leadership development plan. Self-assessments, peer feedback, and reflective practices can provide valuable insight into where an educator excels and where they can improve.

- **Strengths to Build On:**

For instance, a faculty member might have a **strong learning management system (LMS) structure** or excel in providing **empathetic feedback** to students.

- **Areas for Improvement:**

    Common growth areas might include **clearer communication boundaries** (such as establishing expectations for response times) or **creating more student leadership opportunities** within course activities.

By acknowledging both strengths and growth areas, faculty can focus on leveraging existing strengths while developing skills that are critical to their evolving leadership role.

4. Short-Term Goals (1 Semester)

Short-term goals should focus on specific, achievable objectives that can be completed within one semester. These goals provide momentum and create opportunities for immediate improvements.

- **Example Goals:**
    - Introduce **weekly video check-ins** to increase instructor presence and foster more personal connections with students.

- Redesign **peer review assignments** to emphasize collaboration and feedback skills rather than just assessment.
- **Add a mid-semester feedback survey** focused on leadership and support to gauge student perceptions and improve the course experience.

These short-term goals allow for incremental progress, providing an opportunity to test and refine leadership strategies in real-time.

5. Long-Term Goals (1-2 Years)

Long-term goals reflect the broader, more ambitious aspirations for leadership development and teaching excellence. These goals should be aligned with institutional objectives and faculty members' career aspirations.

- **Example Goals:**
  - Facilitate a **faculty workshop on servant leadership** in online teaching, sharing insights and best practices with colleagues.
  - Publish an article or **blog post** about the faculty member's leadership journey and its connection to servant leadership.

- o **Mentor new online instructors** in applying servant leadership principles within their courses, supporting the next generation of educators.

These long-term goals help faculty focus on broader, systemic impact—whether through sharing knowledge, influencing peers, or contributing to the broader educational community.

6. Action Steps and Resources

Each goal should be paired with **actionable steps** that outline how to achieve it. These steps break down the broader goals into smaller, more manageable tasks. Additionally, identifying needed resources (training, peer support, or materials) is crucial to achieving these goals.

Example Goal:

- **Goal:** Create inclusive course announcements.
- **Action Steps:**
    a. Audit existing announcements for tone and inclusivity.
    b. Attend a webinar on inclusive communication.
    c. Draft templates for welcoming, affirming weekly messages to students.

By breaking down each goal into steps and outlining necessary resources, faculty can more easily track their progress and stay motivated.

7. Reflection and Check-In Schedule

Regular **reflection** and **check-ins** are essential to ensure the plan remains dynamic and responsive to changes in the faculty member's leadership journey. Setting a schedule for revisiting the plan allows faculty to assess their progress, adjust strategies, and refine goals.

Reflection Prompts:

- What progress have I made toward my goals?
- What adjustments are needed to better align with my leadership values?
- How has my understanding of servant leadership evolved in practice?

Regular check-ins allow faculty to reflect on their successes, identify areas of struggle, and revise their approach to stay aligned with their mission.

Creating a Personal Servant Leadership Development Plan is an ongoing, evolving process that empowers faculty to be intentional about their leadership growth. This plan fosters a deeper understanding of their mission as educators and leaders, guiding them to make decisions that are not only effective but rooted in values like empathy, equity, and collaboration.

By setting specific goals, identifying strengths and growth areas, and committing to continuous reflection, faculty can continuously refine their leadership practices and enhance the student experience.

Ultimately, the servant leadership development plan serves as a map for ongoing professional and personal growth, ensuring that faculty remain true to their values and continue to evolve as impactful, student-centered leaders.

Template: Personal Servant Leadership Development Plan

Section	Content
Mission Statement	"To support student growth through empathy and integrity..."
Core Values	Equity, Listening, Curiosity, Trust
Strengths	Consistent feedback, approachable tone
Growth Areas	Time management, fostering student collaboration

Short-Term Goals	Pilot reflection threads, record weekly video messages
Long-Term Goals	Mentor peers, lead servant leadership faculty circle
Resources	Books, webinars, peer dialogue, institutional support
Check-In Dates	Monthly journal entries; midterm evaluation

Integrating the Plan Into Professional Practice

This development plan can support promotion portfolios, teaching statements, annual reviews, or peer mentoring relationships. Faculty may also share parts of their plan with students, modeling intentional leadership development and inviting accountability.

Instructors who lead transparently not only elevate their own practice but inspire their students to do the same. They create learning communities rooted in authenticity, care, and ethical aspiration.

In closing, servant leadership is sustained not just through outward actions but through inward discipline. Faculty who reflect regularly, assess thoughtfully, and plan with intention deepen their influence in the classroom and beyond. They become exemplars of the kind of leadership the next generation needs: empathetic, adaptable, grounded in values, and committed to the growth of others.

The next chapter will offer tools, templates, and curated resources that help faculty continue their leadership journey with confidence, creativity, and support.

Chapter 6: Resources, Tools, and Templates for Immediate Use

For faculty committed to integrating servant leadership into their online classrooms, having accessible, practical tools can make the difference between intention and implementation.

While chapters up to this point have focused on the philosophy and practices of leadership in online higher education, this chapter serves as a companion toolbox. It provides ready-to-use resources, sample materials, and guidance for immediate application.

These tools are designed to be adaptable across disciplines and course levels, giving educators the flexibility to tailor them to their unique teaching contexts.

Whether you are revising your course design, creating discussion prompts, or supporting student reflection, the following materials are intended to save time, increase intentionality, and amplify impact.

Servant Leadership Reading and Video Resources

Servant leadership is a powerful and evolving philosophy, offering a compelling model of leadership that emphasizes empathy, community-building, and putting the needs of others first. To deepen both faculty and student understanding of this philosophy, a variety of foundational and contemporary resources can be utilized. These materials will provide insights into the principles, practices, and impact of servant leadership in various contexts, from educational settings to business and beyond.

Books and Articles

- One of the seminal texts on servant leadership is Robert Greenleaf's *The Servant as Leader* (1970). This essay is considered the cornerstone of the servant leadership movement, offering a profound perspective on leadership where the focus shifts from personal ambition to the growth and well-being of others.

- Greenleaf's concept challenges traditional views of leadership, suggesting that the best leaders are those who serve others, thereby enhancing the development of individuals, organizations, and communities.

- Larry Spears' *"Ten Characteristics of the Servant-Leader"* (1995) expands on Greenleaf's foundational ideas, providing a practical breakdown of key servant leadership traits. These characteristics, such as listening, empathy, stewardship, and commitment to the growth of people, form a roadmap for how individuals can embody servant leadership in their professional and personal lives.

- James C. Hunter's *The Servant: A Simple Story About the True Essence of Leadership* (1998) offers an accessible, narrative-based exploration of servant leadership. Through the story of a struggling executive, Hunter conveys how servant leadership can transform individuals and organizations by shifting the focus from authority to service.

- In the academic realm, Laub's *"Assessing the Servant Organization"* (1999) provides critical insights into measuring servant leadership within organizations, particularly educational institutions. It highlights how a commitment to servant leadership can be integrated into organizational culture and how its effectiveness can be assessed through student and faculty experiences.

Videos and Talks

For those seeking a more engaging, multimedia approach to servant leadership, several videos and talks can be valuable resources.

- Simon Sinek's *"Servant Leadership: Putting Your Team First"* (available on YouTube) offers a concise and engaging overview of servant leadership, highlighting how leaders can build stronger teams by focusing on service and the well-being of others. Sinek's compelling narrative brings the principles of servant leadership to life, making them accessible to a broad audience.
- The Greenleaf Center for Servant Leadership (greenleaf.org) is another excellent source for videos, webinars, interviews, and keynote speeches. This resource offers a variety of content that explores servant leadership from different angles, providing insights from thought leaders and practitioners in the field.
- Additionally, TEDx talks on topics such as "leading with empathy" or "inclusive leadership" are rich in content for both students and faculty. These talks offer a contemporary view of servant leadership, demonstrating its relevance in diverse contexts like business, education, and social movements.

These resources can be integrated into course materials to support deeper exploration of servant leadership principles. Faculty can use them in introductory modules, link them to specific assignments, or encourage students to watch and reflect on them as part of their learning journey.

Leadership-Building Discussion Prompts

Discussion boards offer an invaluable opportunity to reflect on and practice leadership. By prompting students to think critically about their leadership experiences, values, and aspirations, these forums foster the development of important leadership skills such as empathy, ethical decision-making, and community-building. Below are several discussion prompts that faculty can use to encourage leadership awareness in students, prompting them to reflect on both their personal experiences and broader leadership principles.

Foundational Prompts

One foundational prompt might ask students to share their experiences with leadership by reflecting on a time when someone's leadership had a positive impact on them. Asking them to consider what qualities made that leadership effective encourages the identification of key traits such as empathy, vision, and ethical behavior.

Another question to deepen their understanding of leadership might be: *"How would you define ethical leadership in your future career field?"* This prompt encourages students to connect abstract leadership principles with their professional aspirations and the ethical challenges they may face in their fields.

Exploring the difference between power and influence is also a key leadership concept. A discussion prompt such as: *"What is the difference between power and influence in leadership?"* can help students recognize the importance of non-coercive, relational influence in servant leadership.

Applied Prompts

Applied prompts encourage students to connect leadership theories to their own lived experiences. For example, after working on group projects, students could reflect on their role in the team, responding to a prompt like: *"Reflect on a group experience. How did you contribute to its success or challenge as a leader or team member?"* This prompt invites students to evaluate their leadership behaviors in the context of collaboration, helping them understand how their actions impact others.

In more complex leadership scenarios, students might be prompted to consider crisis management through the lens of servant leadership: *"If you were tasked with leading a crisis response, what servant leadership traits would guide your decisions?"* This type of prompt encourages critical thinking about how servant leadership principles—such as empathy, stewardship, and commitment to the growth of others—apply to high-pressure situations.

Additionally, a prompt such as: *"Who do you lead right now, even informally? What responsibility comes with that influence?"* encourages students to examine informal leadership roles they may occupy in their communities, workplaces, or families, reinforcing the idea that leadership is not just for formal positions but is a part of everyday interactions.

Reflective Prompts

Reflective prompts give students an opportunity to assess their own leadership development and identify areas of growth. For instance, asking students: *"What leadership traits are you currently developing, and what is challenging about them?"* provides insight into how they view their leadership journey and what obstacles they may be facing.

Another reflective prompt might be: *"In what ways do you build or harm community in your online interactions?"* This question invites students to examine how their behaviors contribute to the sense of community in an online learning environment and how servant leadership principles can foster positive interactions.

Finally, a reflective prompt such as: *"Which of the 10 servant leadership characteristics do you most identify with and why?"* encourages students to delve into the specific traits of servant leadership that resonate with them personally, helping them see how they can embody these characteristics in their lives.

Faculty can rotate prompts each week or allow students to choose from a list, offering flexibility and encouraging deeper engagement with the material. By incorporating multimedia responses—such as videos, written reflections, or creative presentations—students can engage with these prompts in a variety of ways, promoting diverse perspectives and creativity in their learning.

Course Announcement Templates

Effective course announcements serve more than a logistical function; they help create a sense of community, inspire students, and reinforce the course's leadership development goals. Below are templates for different stages of the course that faculty can use to create announcements that align with servant leadership principles.

Welcome Announcement

Subject: *Welcome to Our Course & Learning Community!*

"Hello everyone,

Welcome to [Course Name]! I'm excited to guide you through a learning experience focused not only on subject mastery but also on leadership development. Each of you brings unique insights and strengths to this space, and I look forward to learning from you as well.

As we begin, please take a few minutes to introduce yourself in the 'Getting to Know You' forum. Let's start building a learning community where support, respect, and curiosity thrive.

Looking forward to our journey,

[Your Name]"

Mid-Semester Encouragement

Subject: *You're Growing—and I See It*

"Hi everyone,

As we reach the midpoint of the term, I want to take a moment to acknowledge your progress. Leadership is often about quiet consistency, and I see so many of you showing up, supporting peers, and diving into meaningful reflection. Remember, growth isn't always linear, and leadership isn't about perfection. Keep going—and don't hesitate to reach out if you need support.

Gratefully,

[Your Name]"

Closing Message

Subject: *Looking Back—and Looking Ahead*

"Dear all,

As we wrap up the course, I'm deeply proud of the way this class has evolved. Thank you for engaging with the content and one another so fully. I hope you leave with not just new knowledge but a deeper sense of who you are as a leader. Please take a moment to complete the course reflection activity and, if you feel inclined, send a note about what this course meant to you.

Wishing you continued growth,

[Your Name]"

These announcements offer students not only information about the course but also affirm their growth and leadership journey. They serve to strengthen community, encourage reflection, and maintain a focus on leadership throughout the course.

Activity and Assignment Instructions

Here are sample overviews and instructions for key servant leadership-focused activities.

Activity: Peer Leadership Forum Rotation

Overview: Each week, a student will serve as the discussion leader. They will post a prompt, engage peers, and provide a summary.

Instructions:

1. Review the assigned reading.
2. Post a discussion question by Monday.
3. Respond to at least three classmates by Thursday.
4. Post a 1-paragraph summary by Sunday.

Evaluation Criteria: Engagement, originality, tone, and synthesis.

Assignment: Leadership Reflection Journal

Overview: This ongoing journal invites you to reflect on your growth as a servant leader.

Instructions:

1. Post one entry per week (200–300 words).
2. Use the provided prompts or choose your own.

3. Optional: Respond to a peer's reflection each week.

Grading: Completion, thoughtfulness, and evidence of personal insight.

Simulation: Crisis Leadership Scenario

Overview: Work in teams to respond to a fictional campus crisis from a leadership role.

Instructions:

1. Review your team's role and the crisis briefing.
2. Prepare a written response or video statement.
3. Submit by Sunday and complete a team debrief.

Evaluation: Clarity, ethics, teamwork, and application of servant leadership principles.

Student Leadership Self-Assessment and Reflection Forms

These forms provide students with a structured way to evaluate and articulate their leadership development over time.

Self-Assessment Form (Likert scale: 1 = rarely to 5 = consistently)

- I listen carefully to peers and instructors.

- I show empathy in my communication.
- I offer constructive feedback and encouragement.
- I take initiative in group tasks.
- I reflect on my values and apply them to decisions.
- I support a positive learning environment.

Optional Reflection Questions:

- What are your top 2 leadership strengths right now?
- What is one area you want to grow in?
- Describe a moment this term where you acted as a leader.

End-of-Course Reflection Prompt

"Looking back at the course, how have you grown as a leader? What practices will you carry with you into future roles?"

By incorporating these tools into their courses, faculty equip themselves and their students for meaningful, values-based engagement. Servant leadership is not built through occasional big moments but through the daily choices that prioritize service, empathy, and growth. With these resources, faculty can lead with intention and empower students to do the same.

Chapter 7: Voices from the Field: Faculty and Leadership Educator Perspectives

While theory and structured practices provide the foundation for servant leadership in online higher education, there is unparalleled value in hearing from those actively navigating this work in real classrooms. This chapter brings together voices from experienced online faculty and leadership educators to highlight the human side of leadership in virtual spaces. Through curated interviews, key takeaways, and brief case vignettes, we explore what servant leadership looks like in practice—with all its nuance, creativity, and real-world application.

These stories ground servant leadership in context. They demonstrate how instructors build trust, encourage growth, and model ethical leadership amid the complexities of asynchronous teaching. They offer wisdom, challenges, and inspiration from those deeply committed to fostering student-centered, values-based learning environments.

Case Studies

Case Study 1: Whitney Oliver, MBA, lecturer at East Tennessee State University's College of Public Health

Recognized for her servant leadership approach to online teaching, where the heart of education is empathy, connection, and meaningful engagement.

Oliver views online education as more than content delivery; for her, it's about cultivating human connection. *"While content is important, empathy and intentional connection are what truly make learning stick,"* she explained. This people-centered philosophy earned her the inaugural Online Teaching Award from ETSU's Center for Teaching Excellence.

Though her career began in elementary education and later in healthcare process improvement, Oliver found herself drawn back to teaching — this time, with a focus on adult learners in higher education. She now blends her backgrounds in education and health care to prepare students for the workforce.

Oliver embodies a servant leader's mindset, prioritizing the needs of her students and community. *"I believe that educational practice must be flexible, reflective and responsive to the evolving needs of students and society,"* she shares. Through community-engaged learning, students tackle real-world challenges with local organizations, gaining both professional and personal growth.

Her leadership philosophy pushes students toward growth by encouraging resilience and adaptability. *"Above all, I encourage my students to 'get comfortable being uncomfortable,' pushing them beyond their comfort zones to discover their potential and embrace lifelong learning,"* Oliver emphasized.

Key Insights:

Empathy and Connection Matter: Oliver stresses that meaningful online learning hinges on empathy and intentional connection, not just content delivery.

Servant Leadership Philosophy: Her teaching style reflects servant leadership values — prioritizing student needs, fostering professional growth, and supporting community partnerships.

Continuous Improvement: Oliver emphasizes that teaching should be **flexible, reflective, and responsive** to both students and societal needs.

Community-Engaged Learning: She integrates practical problem-solving with local organizations, connecting coursework to real-world challenges.

Lifelong Learning Mindset: Oliver encourages students to embrace discomfort as a path to growth, preparing them for the complexities of professional life.

Recognition for Impactful Online Teaching: Oliver's people-first, servant-leader approach earned ETSU's inaugural Online Teaching Award.

Case Study 2: Dr. Anya Sharma - Navigating Global Ethics

Dr. Anya Sharma teaches "Global Ethical Leadership," an online graduate course. Recognizing that students in an online environment might feel isolated, she consciously adopts a servant leadership approach, emphasizing connection, intellectual stimulation, and personal growth. She views her role less as the central authority figure ("sage on the stage") and more as a "guide on the side", facilitating student discovery and dialogue. Dr. Sharma believes that the asynchronous nature of online learning, while posing challenges, also provides a unique venue for fostering deep reflection and critical thinking, key components of both ethical leadership and transformative learning.

Her servant leadership is evident in several ways. She prioritizes **wisdom** and **persuasive mapping**, structuring discussions around complex ethical dilemmas students are likely to face in their careers. Instead of simply providing answers, she uses discussion forums to guide students to analyze situations from multiple perspectives, encouraging them to build and share their own insights through collaborative dialogue. She frequently poses questions that challenge assumptions and require students to reflect critically on ethical frameworks. When debates arise, she employs persuasive mapping to help students understand different viewpoints and navigate towards reasoned conclusions, demonstrating patience and pedagogy.

Dr. Sharma also focuses on **altruistic calling**, a key predictor of student satisfaction. She is highly available to students, offering detailed, personalized feedback on assignments and proactively checking in with those who seem less engaged. She sees her work as a special calling, measuring success by the growth and success of her students. She encourages students to ask questions without stress and is willing to provide extra time to help them understand complex ethical concepts. This commitment to their individual growth goes beyond the required tasks, fostering a sense of care and personal consideration.

In promoting **awareness**, Dr. Sharma incorporates activities that require students to evaluate online sources critically. She understands that in the digital age, information literacy skills are crucial for discerning quality and credibility. She explicitly discusses the challenges of navigating online content and helps students develop the competencies to do so effectively.

While the source doesn't detail specific outcomes for this fictional professor, research indicates that instructors demonstrating altruistic calling, persuasive mapping, and wisdom tend to have more satisfied students in online settings. By focusing on these attributes, Dr. Sharma likely enhances student satisfaction, engagement, and the development of critical ethical reasoning skills. Her approach also aligns with the idea that online learning can be innovative and personally transformative when built on trust and shared values.

Key Insights:

- **Focusing on specific servant leadership attributes like wisdom, persuasive mapping, and altruistic calling** is crucial for online instructors to enhance student satisfaction and guide them through complex subject matter.
- An online servant leader acts as a guide who facilitates dialogue and critical reflection, leveraging online tools

like discussion forums to promote collaborative knowledge building and the challenging of assumptions.

- Helping students develop information literacy and critical evaluation skills is an important aspect of an online servant leader's role in promoting awareness and responsible engagement with digital content.

Case Study 3: Prof. Ben Carter - Building Community in Online Organizational Behavior

Prof. Ben Carter teaches an undergraduate online course titled "Introduction to Organizational Behavior." He is acutely aware that online learners can experience social isolation and aims to build a strong sense of **community** and **belonging**. He believes that fostering a supportive online community is essential for student engagement and success.

Prof. Carter explicitly uses online forums and small group spaces to encourage interaction. Drawing on studies that highlight the importance of trust in online communities, he dedicates time at the beginning of the course to establish clear guidelines for online communication and interaction, promoting a trustful environment. He explains the rules and procedures for online discussions, empowering students to participate effectively.

He acts as a **facilitator**, initially leading discussions, then supporting and empowering students, eventually stepping back to intervene only when necessary. He actively calls out silent students in discussions, employing a form of "shepherd leadership" to ensure everyone feels included and encouraged to participate. By fostering interdependency, he encourages students to rely on each other, identifying knowledge gaps and asking peers for help.

Prof. Carter incorporates activities designed to build **emotional healing** and empathy, two characteristics of servant leadership. While emotional healing didn't significantly predict satisfaction in one study, the sources suggest it is a key servant leadership behavior. He encourages students to share relevant personal experiences related to course topics (like team dynamics or leadership challenges) in a designated "sharing corner" forum, fostering empathy and understanding among peers. He responds empathetically to students facing personal challenges, recognizing the demands of busy working/family lives that many ODL students face.

He structures assignments, like group projects managed within online small group spaces, to require collaboration and shared responsibility. As students achieve joint successes, their willingness to share and engage in public forums increases, building trust and a unified voice. This reciprocity in communication binds learners together.

Based on the sources, building community can enhance e-learner engagement and motivation. Prof. Carter's focus on fostering trust, encouraging peer interaction, and acting as a compassionate facilitator contributes to creating a vibrant online learning community where students feel a sense of belonging, potentially counteracting the challenges of social isolation.

Key Insights:

- **Building community and fostering a sense of belonging** are critical applications of servant leadership in the online classroom, helping to combat student isolation and enhance engagement.

- Online instructors can build trust and empower students by setting clear communication guidelines, acting as facilitators, and proactively encouraging participation, including reaching out to less active students.

- Creating opportunities for peer interaction and interdependency in collaborative activities strengthens the online community and motivates students to engage more deeply.

Case Study 4: Dr. Clara Evans - Servant Leadership in Action

Dr. Clara Evans teaches an upper-level online course, "Servant Leadership in Practice," designed for emergency services majors. The course specifically explores applying servant leadership principles within professional contexts, moving beyond theoretical understanding to practical application and personal development. She aims for students to not only understand the concepts but to internalize them and aspire to become servant leaders themselves.

Dr. Evans models **commitment to the growth of others** and **stewardship,** particularly through a significant course project inspired by the concept of community service learning. Students are tasked with designing and implementing a small online initiative to support a community group (e.g., developing a public safety awareness campaign for the elderly or creating online resources for local volunteers). Dr. Evans acts as a coach and advisor, helping students navigate the project challenges and reflect on how their academic skills can benefit others. This "Charity Community Service course" model provides a window into real-world experience and promotes a sense of social responsibility.

She encourages **transformative learning** by requiring students to maintain a weekly eJournal. In these journals, students reflect deeply on the course readings and their project experiences, connecting the concepts of servant leadership to their own lives and career aspirations. Dr. Evans provides thoughtful, personalized feedback on these journals, helping students become critically aware of their assumptions and facilitating their personal growth journeys.

She leverages various online resources, including research papers and other online applications, integrating them into the course. Her teaching style is highly relational; she focuses on **listening** and **empathy**, making herself available via Skype and email for individual supervision and support, akin to being an "empowering peer/coach". She pays close attention to student writings, identifying moments of personal reflection and understanding.

A qualitative case study involving a similar course found that it left lasting impressions on students' understanding of leadership and reinforced their desire to become servant leaders. Dr. Evans' approach, by integrating service learning and deep personal reflection facilitated by servant leadership principles, aims to achieve similar outcomes, connecting theoretical knowledge to practical application and fostering the student's natural desire to serve. The use of reflective eJournals in a distance learning format was found to be effective in allowing students to explore the theory independently and connect it to their lived experience.

Key Insights:

- Integrating **community service learning** projects into online courses, facilitated by a servant leader, can effectively connect academic knowledge to real-world application and foster students' sense of social responsibility and motivation.

- Utilizing tools like **online journals or blogs** for personal reflection, coupled with empathetic feedback from the instructor, supports **transformative learning** and helps students internalize servant leadership principles.

- An online servant leader focuses on the **growth of others**, acting as a coach and guide to help students achieve their potential, including applying their skills to benefit society.

Key Takeaways, Strategies, and Leadership Moments

Across these case studies, several key themes emerged that are consistent with servant leadership values and practices:

1. Leadership Is Relational and Present

In every interview, presence came up as a core concept. Not presence in the traditional, physical sense, but in how instructors show up through:

- Timely responses
- Empathetic messages
- Personalized feedback
- Predictable communication rhythms

2. Vulnerability Builds Trust

Faculty who are willing to be vulnerable—to share their struggles, admit mistakes, or name their emotions—create space for student trust and authenticity. Vulnerability, far from being a weakness, becomes a leadership asset.

3. Leadership Is Modeled in Small Acts

Micro-leadership practices, like affirming a student's effort, using inclusive language, or adjusting a policy to honor compassion, were frequently cited. These acts embody servant leadership more powerfully than broad declarations.

4. Students Must Be Invited Into Leadership

A recurring strategy was creating formal structures that empower students to lead:

- Peer facilitation

- Group project roles
- Student-led reflections
- Leadership journals

Faculty emphasized the need to support and scaffold these experiences so students feel safe to step up.

5. Reflection Drives Growth

Instructors stressed the importance of reflection for both themselves and their students. Reflective prompts, journals, and end-of-module check-ins help crystallize learning and reinforce leadership mindsets.

Conclusion

This book began with a premise rooted in hope: that leadership, especially the servant kind, is not limited to titles or boardrooms, nor is it constrained by time zones, screens, or course syllabi. It lives in daily decisions—in how faculty show up, support, and shape the learning environments entrusted to them.

In the evolving landscape of online higher education, servant leadership is both a mindset and a method. It is a call to prioritize empathy over efficiency, community over content delivery, and transformation over transaction. Through the chapters in this volume, we have explored what it means to lead online with integrity, humility, and care.

We examined the foundations of servant leadership and how they intersect with the unique demands of asynchronous instruction. We explored how course design, announcements, feedback, and group structures can all serve as platforms for leadership development—for both faculty and students. We engaged with faculty voices, reflections, and real-life examples that brought theory to life. And we provided practical tools, prompts, and templates to make implementation immediate and meaningful.

What emerges is a clear narrative: servant leadership is not an abstract theory but an actionable ethos. It is deeply needed in today's educational ecosystems, where human connection must be intentionally fostered amid digital complexity. It empowers instructors to be more than content experts; it calls them to be mentors, facilitators, and co-learners.

To the educators reading this: your leadership matters. The space you hold for your students, the presence you establish in your virtual classrooms, the compassion you infuse into your emails, policies, and grading—these are the seeds of transformation. They shape not only student success but student character.

To those seeking to take the next step: revisit the reflection prompts, activity guides, and assessment tools offered throughout this book.

Use them not only to evaluate your students but to evaluate yourself.

Leadership begins within.

Finally, remember that this journey is ongoing. There is no finish line for servant leadership. It is a cycle of reflection, learning, humility, and service.

But in walking this path, you do more than teach. You build futures. You grow leaders.

And in a world increasingly shaped by remote interaction, that kind of leadership—grounded in empathy, fueled by purpose, and sustained through service—has never been more essential.

Thank you for leading boldly, and thank you for leading well.

Appendix

Foundational Works on Servant Leadership

Autry, J. A (2004). *The Servant Leader: How to Build a Creative Team, Develop Great Moral, and Improve Bottom-Line Performance.* Currency: New York.

Blanchard, K. and Broadwell, R. (xxxx). Servant Leadership in Action.

Blanchard, K., Hodges, P., & Hendry, J. (2003). *The servant leader: Transforming your heart, head, hands, & habits.* Thomas Nelson.

Greenleaf, R. K. (1977). *Servant leadership: A journey into the nature of legitimate power and greatness.* Paulist Press.

Keith, K. M. (2008). *The case for servant leadership.* Greenleaf Center for Servant Leadership.

Kouzes, J. and Posner, B. (2023). *The Leadership Challenge.* Jossey-Bass.

Lencioni, P. (2002) *The Five Dysfunctions of a Team.* Jossey-Bass.

Sinek, S. (2017) *Leaders Eat Last.* Portfolio.

Sipe, J. W., & Frick, D. M. (2009). *Seven pillars of servant leadership: Practicing the wisdom of leading by serving.* Paulist Press.

Spears, L. C. (Ed.). (1995). *Reflections on leadership: How Robert K. Greenleaf's theory of servant leadership influenced today's top management thinkers.* John Wiley & Sons.

Theoretical and Conceptual Explorations

Chiniara, M., & Bentein, K. (2016). Linking servant leadership to individual performance: Differentiating the mediating role of autonomy, competence, and relatedness need satisfaction. *The Leadership Quarterly, 27*(1), 124-141. https://doi.org/10.1016/j.leaqua.2015.08.004

Eva, N., Robin, M., Sendjaya, S., van Dierendonck, D., & Liden, R. C. (2019). Servant leadership: A systematic review and call for future research. *The Leadership Quarterly, 30*(1), 111-132. https://doi.org/10.1016/j.leaqua.2018.07.004

Lemoine, G. J., Hartnell, C. A., & Leroy, H. (2019). Taking stock of moral approaches to leadership: An integrative review of ethical, authentic, and servant leadership. *Academy of Management Annals, 13*(1), 148-187. https://doi.org/10.5465/annals.2016.0121

Liden, R. C., Wayne, S. J., Zhao, H., & Henderson, D. (2008). Servant leadership: Development of a multidimensional measure and multi-level assessment. *The Leadership Quarterly, 19*(2), 161-177. https://doi.org/10.1016/j.leaqua.2008.01.006

Panaccio, A., Henderson, D. J., Liden, R. C., Wayne, S. J., & Cao, X. (2015). Toward an understanding of when and why servant leadership accounts for employee extra-role behaviors. *Journal of Business Psychology, 30*(4), 657-675. https://doi.org/10.1007/s10869-014-9388-z

Empirical Studies and Applications

van Dierendonck, D. (2011). Servant leadership: A review and synthesis. *Journal of Management, 37*(4), 1228-1261. https://doi.org/10.1177/0149206310380462

Servant Leadership in Contemporary Contexts

Sendjaya, S., & Sarros, J. C. (2002). Servant leadership: Its origin, development, and application in organizations. *Journal of Leadership & Organizational Studies, 9*(2), 57-64. https://doi.org/10.1177/107179190200900205

Servant Leadership in Online Education

Ali, A., & Ahmad, I. (2011). Key factors for determining students' satisfaction in distance learning courses: A study of Allama Iqbal Open University. Contemporary Educational Technology, 2(2), 118-134.

Barnabas, A., Joseph, A., & Clifford, P. (2010). The need for awareness of servant leadership in business schools. Academic Leadership (15337812), 8(2), 1-6.

Black, G. (2010). Correlational analysis of servant leadership and school climate. Catholic Education: A Journal of Inquiry & Practice, 13(4), 437-466.

Bogler, R., Caspi, A., & Roccas, S. (2013). Transformational and passive leadership: An initial investigation of university instructors as leaders in a virtual learning environment. Educational Management Administration & Leadership, 41(3), 372-392. doi:10.1177/1741143212474805

Bolkan, S., & Goodboy, A. K. (2011). Behavioral Indicators of Transformational Leadership in the College Classroom. Qualitative Research Reports In Communication, 12(1), 10-18. doi:10.1080/17459435.2011.601520

Bolkan, J. (2013). Report: Students taking online courses jumps 96 percent over 5 years. Campus Technology. Retrieved from http://campustechnology.com/articles/ 2013/06/24/report-students-taking-online-courses-jumps-96-percent-over-5-years.aspx

Bowen, W.G. (2013). Walk deliberately, don't run, toward online education. The Chronicle of Higher Education. Retrieved from http://chronicle.com/article/Walk-Deliberately-Dont-Run/138109/

Buchen, I. H. (1998). Servant leadership: A model for future faculty and future institutions. The Journal of Leadership Studies, 5(1), 125-134.

Bryant, C., & Nieves, J. (2012). A case study of the effectiveness of WebCT As a student-learning tool for the Introduction to Servant Leadership class.

Cole, M. T., Shelley, D. J., & Swartz, L. B. (2014). Online instruction, e-learning, and student satisfaction: A three year study. International Review Of Research In Open & Distance Learning, 15(6), 111-131.

Crippen, C. (2010). Serve, teach, and lead: It's all about relationships. *Insight: A Journal of Scholarly Teaching, 5*, 27-36.

Croxton, R. A. (2014). The role of interactivity in student satisfaction and persistence in online learning. Journal Of Online Learning & Teaching, 10(2), 314-324.

Digo, G. S. (2021). Servant leadership of graduate students: Basis for the development of online distance course. *ASEAN Journal of Open and Online Distance Education, 13*(2), 104-118.

Hart, C. (2012). Factors associated with student persistence in an online program of study: A review of the literature. Journal Of Interactive Online Learning, 11(1), 19-42.

Hazel, M., Crandall, H. M., & Caputo, J. S. (2014). The influence of instructor social presence and student academic entitlement on teacher misbehaviors in online courses. Southern Communication Journal, 79(4), 311-326. doi:10.1080/1041794X.2014.914563

Hill, T. & Lewicki, P. (2007). Statistics: Methods and applications. StatSoft, Tulsa, OK.

Huber, R. L. (2014). Servant leadership, self-efficacy, and communities of inquiry in higher education online learning (Order No. 3623182). Available from

ProQuest Dissertations & Theses Full Text. (1548333568). Retrieved from http://search.proquest.com.proxy1.ncu.edu/docview/1548333568/58B40E1F1D84EC1PQ/6?accountid=28180#

Huber, R. & Carter, H. (2014). Applying the Servant Leadership Model to E-Teaching. In T. Bastiaens (Ed.), *Proceedings of World Conference on E-Learning* (pp. 880-887). New Orleans, LA, USA: Association for the Advancement of Computing in Education (AACE). Retrieved May 21, 2025 from https://www.learntechlib.org/p/148968.

Roberts, J. (May 13, 2025) "Creating connection in virtual classrooms," Elizabethton Star. Retrieved from: https://elizabethton.com/2025/05/13/creating-connection-in-virtual-classrooms/

Russell, E. J. (2013). Servant leadership through distance learning: A case study. *Turkish Online Journal of Distance Education, 14*(4), 26-45.

Sahawneh, F.G. & Benuto, L.T. (2018). The relationship between instructor servant leadership behaviors and satisfaction with instructors in an online setting.

Online Learning, 22(1), 107-129. doi:10.24059/olj.v22i1.1066.

Tucker, B. (2023). *The Effects of Instructor Servant Leadership Traits on Student Satisfaction in Online Education at Non-Profit Institutions* (Doctoral dissertation, University of the Cumberlands).

van de Bunt-Kokhuis, S. G. M., & Sultan, N. (2012). Servant-leadership: the Online Way! E-learning where community building is key. *European Journal of Open, Distance and E-learning, 472.*

van de Bunt-Kokhuis, S. Enhancing social justice in e-learning by servant-leadership.

Wheeler, D. W. (2012). Servant leadership for higher education: Principles and practices. San Francisco, CA: Wiley

Woodall, T., Hiller, A., & Resnick, S. (2014). Making sense of higher education: students as consumers and the value of the university experience. Studies In Higher Education, 39(1), 48-67. doi:10.1080/03075079.2011.648373

Xu, D., & Jaggars, S. S. (2011). The effectiveness of distance education across Virginia's community colleges: Evidence from introductory college-level math and

English courses. *Educational Evaluation And Policy Analysis, 33*(3), 360-377. doi:10.3102/0162373711413814

About the Author

Dr. David McNamee is a dedicated educator, passionate leader, and lifelong learner with a rich and diverse background. He serves as a Professor of Leadership in the MS in Leadership program at the University of Arkansas Grantham. His influence extends globally as an international faculty with Jesuit Worldwide Learning and as a Senior Fellow with Co-Serve International, where he continues to share his expertise in leadership and service. Read more at https://www.drdavidmcnamee.com/. Please consider following me and posting reviews of my work at Amazon.

About Sage Quill Press

Sage Quill Press is dedicated to publishing works that inspire, educate, and empower individuals and organizations through the principles of servant leadership. We curate and publish insightful books, scholarly research, and thought-provoking papers that foster ethical leadership, personal growth, and transformative service at https://sagequillpress.com/

Also by David McNamee

Did you love *Elevating Education: A Servant Leadership Approach for Online Educators?* Then you should read <u>Servant Leadership: Lessons for Middle School Students</u> 2nd ed. by David McNamee and Daniel G. McNamee!

Education has evolved, and so has this book, expanding beyond its original scope to influence teacher certification programs worldwide. Leadership isn't about authority. It's about service, empathy, and empowering others. Middle schoolers may not hold formal leadership roles, but they influence their peers daily. By fostering collaboration, trust, and ethical decision-making, we prepare them to lead with integrity. With examples for Administrators, Teachers, and Instructional Coaches, this updated edition equips educators with practical strategies, real-world examples, and interactive activities to nurture servant leadership in students. As they learn to lead by serving, educators reflect on their leadership practices because the best leaders lead by example.

www.ingramcontent.com/pod-product-compliance
Lightning Source LLC
Chambersburg PA
CBHW070141100426
42743CB00013B/2785